Little Laureates

Highlands & Islands

Edited by Heather Killingray

First published in Great Britain in 2007 by:
Young Writers
Remus House
Coltsfoot Drive
Peterborough
PE2 9JX
Telephone: 01733 890066
Website: www.youngwriters.co.uk

SB ISBN 978-1 84602 999 8

Foreword

Young Writers was established in 1991 and has been passionately devoted to the promotion of reading and writing in children and young adults ever since. The quest continues today. Young Writers remains as committed to the nurturing of poetic and literary talent as ever.

This year's Young Writers competition has proven as vibrant and dynamic as ever and we are delighted to present a showcase of the best poetry from across the UK and in some cases overseas. Each poem has been selected from a wealth of *Little Laureates* entries before ultimately being published in this, our sixteenth primary school poetry series.

Once again, we have been supremely impressed by the overall quality of the entries we have received. The imagination, energy and creativity which has gone into each young writer's entry made choosing the poems a challenging and often difficult but ultimately hugely rewarding task - the general high standard of the work submitted ensured this opportunity to bring their poetry to a larger appreciative audience.

We sincerely hope you are pleased with this final collection and that you will enjoy *Little Laureates Highlands & Islands* for many years to come.

Contents

The Poems

My Dog Goldie

My dog Goldie is quite cute,
My dog Goldie loves to chew,
My dog Goldie is never mute,
But my dog Goldie is never blue.

My dog Goldie loves a nap,
Especially when he's on my lap,
He just needs a little bite,
To keep him going through the night.

My dog Goldie's a furry pup,
My dog Goldie's a cheeky pup,
My dog Goldie's a powerful pup,
But he's just a mischievous pup.

My dog Goldie's particularly lazy,
When it's cold and the sun is hazy,
He loves to walk and waggles his tail,
All the way around the trail.

Caitlin Nicolson (11)
Aird Primary School, Isle of Lewis

The Beach

The beach is like a catwalk,
Full of models who strut around,
Hot colours, red, orange and yellow,
Like the fanciest clothes in town.

The sea sparkles and I can see,
Blue, turquoise and green,
Hot sands burn my feet
And people shout and scream.

Games of volleyball, football and frisbee,
Children laughing, having fun,
Swimming like fish and splashing around,
Enjoying the lovely golden sun.

Lydia Clark (11)
Aird Primary School, Isle of Lewis

Lewis Is A Land . . .

Lewis is a land,
Of forest and shore,
It is the land,
That thrills me to the core.

Lewis is a land,
Of peace and tranquillity,
Weather not too great,
But you're always by the sea.

Lewis is a land,
Of moor that never ends,
Villages and small towns
And roads that always bend.

Lewis is a land,
Out in the Hebrides,
It is not too popular,
In the cold North Seas.

Lewis is a land,
That I can't but adore,
I will always love it,
Its moor and rocky shore.

Lewis is a land,
As you now know,
Full of beauty and wonder,
Oh how I love it so.

Stuart Macleod-Lamont (10)
Aird Primary School, Isle of Lewis

Water

Starts in the mountain as a little stream,
Runs down the mountainside and goes with the flow.

Meandering around, crashing about,
Making a mess is the thing it does,
Ox Bow Lake getting made
When you don't know it is.

Water oh so sweet,
Oh how we love it,
How can we live without it?
I do not know.

No water in Africa,
How do they live?
No rain, just sun,
Oh how much they need it.

Alasdair Maciver (9)
Aird Primary School, Isle of Lewis

Scotland!

It's the best place to be,
Fields, beaches, enjoy free,
Climb on all the best trees,
All the juice freshly squeezed.

Ducks swimming in the loch,
Mummy wearing a frilly frock,
My dog running round the beach,
The prettiest flower out of reach.

Wind blowing in my hair,
Green grass everywhere,
Weather's not always good,
But visit Scotland, you really should.

Olivia Woodley (10)
Aird Primary School, Isle of Lewis

Once At Night

Once at night, tired was I,
In my bed quiet as mice,
Noises all around, scary and bright,
Coming from the window over in the light.

Once at night, I was tired,
In came a ghost, and put on the light,
A ghostly figure, oh so pale,
I thought, *what a sight.*

Once at night, the light was on,
In my mirror I had a peek,
Sure enough, a ghost it was,
No reflection, I could seek.

Once at night, it spoke to me,
Softly and sweetly, nice and calm,
A pool for you just wait and see,
Wrapped around your little hand.

Once at night, so excited,
In my head I could picture,
Oh so bright, I can't wait,
Oh I hope, not a mixture.

Once at night, after all that,
He was around for a year,
This night, tonight he must go
And I'll be here all alone.

Kirsty Johnstone (11)
Aird Primary School, Isle of Lewis

A Woeful Night

At night in the dark,
In my bed I shiver,
I hear a dog bark
And the noise makes me quiver.

Outside it looks frightening,
I see the flash of lightning,
Outside the rain is pouring down,
The sound of thunder makes me frown.

There's a moan, there's rain,
The wind is so strong,
The sound is like a pain,
This night is going to take so long.

I can hear a big owl
And then a dog starts to howl,
Then I really get a fright,
I hate this night!

Tonight slates start to fall,
Waves crash, trees shiver,
I can hear a big fall,
Then I start to quiver.

The darkness outside my window,
The stars I cannot see,
But I hope the morning,
Will bring the sunshine to me.

Amanda Nicolson (9)
Aird Primary School, Isle of Lewis

The Magic Mermaid

Today I saw a mermaid,
She jumped out of the sea,
She was so very beautiful,
From her head down to her knee.

She had a pink glittery tail,
That shone from afar,
A big golden ring,
That flashed like a star.

She had a pet sea horse,
As small as can be,
He was a bright blue colour,
That blended with the sea.

One day she met a man
And fell in love with he,
She looked at him every minute,
As he chanted through the sea.

She had a special wand,
That carried lots of magic spells,
There were spells for frogs and spells for hogs
And even one for ringing bells.

Today she saw the human man,
She met the other day,
He asked her for her hand in marriage,
But she had to swim away.

Then she saw a merman as beautiful as could be,
He asked her if she'd marry him
And got down on his knee,
She said yes, he leapt up in joy
And they went dancing through the sea.

Jenny Mactaggart (10)
Aird Primary School, Isle of Lewis

Midnight Monsters

Last night was a noisy night,
Creaks and lightning and wind,
I was really scared with fright,
In case a monster actually came in!

But then I heard the window opening
And heard a little groan,
I saw a tiny green foot, stepping in,
As skinny as a bone.

A tiny little hairy face,
I saw with my own two eyes,
It held a big brown heavy case,
Full of colourful ties.

I thought I was dreaming,
What a strange little man,
His antennae were beaming,
Like the sun in a frying pan.

He said his name was Tiny,
No wonder, he was so small,
We became best friends,
In fact the best of all.

He took me to his own planet,
To show me his home,
He had a small wife called Janet,
She looked very alone.

But then I had to go back,
To planet Earth I was sent,
I'll really, really miss Tiny,
I wish he never went.

Shona Marie Mackinnon (10)
Aird Primary School, Isle of Lewis

My Magic Stone!

My magic stone,
Was once all alone,
Lying on the beach,
Thrown out of the ocean.

Its colours are pink and sparkly,
All the colours I've ever known,
This magic stone,
I could not pawn,
It is all my own.

If I ever lost my magic stone,
I'd be all alone,
I'd moan and groan,
I'd fly around like a cyclone,
Until I'd found
My magic stone!

Aimee Lupton (10)
Aird Primary School, Isle of Lewis

Robot

There once was a robot,
Who didn't know who he was,
So he went to Robotland,
But he soon got banned.

Soon he was wealthy and grand,
But now he has no friends,
Now the road just bends,
No one knows where it ends.

He lost all his land
And demanded it back,
He didn't get it back,
But got a friend called Mack.

Ewen MacBain (10)
Aird Primary School, Isle of Lewis

My Magical Stone

My magical stone grants me wishes,
I wish that it would do the dishes,
I wish it'd hoover and do as it must
And that every room has no dust.

My mum tells me to throw it out,
But I tell her no and give a big shout!
I try and hide it but she always finds it,
Because she just doesn't know when to quit.

My dad always agrees with my mum
And tells her something has to be done,
My dad tries to stomp on it with his big feet,
But he misses it and kicks Mum's seat.

I tell my magical stone,
While I sit on my magic throne,
I have to do jobs for my mum,
That really has to be done.

My mum found out that my stone does the jobs
And she threw my big teddy Mr Blob,
When she found out she gave a big shout
And then threw my magic stone about.

Now she was cursed,
So she gave me the stone first,
Then there was a bright light
And then she turned into a mite.

I was really upset,
Because she hadn't met,
My new friend at school,
Who had a big pool.

Jade Collins (10)
Aird Primary School, Isle of Lewis

If I Were The Sea

How I would love to be the sea,
I would be much stronger than a bee,
I could make humongous waves
And go into hundreds of caves.

I love the colour blue
And I could tell the sky to shoo,
I would crash into rocks,
But I would never hurt a fox.

I would be able to see fish,
But I have a wish,
To see Japan,
Milan and Iran.

I would be very salty,
I wouldn't be faulty,
I don't like it when they drop litter,
It makes me feel bitter.

How I'd love to be the sea,
It would be me, just me.

Andrew Megson (11)
Aird Primary School, Isle of Lewis

My Dog

I have a dog called Max,
He's very old and bold,
He's also very smelly
And deaf because he's old.

My dog Max is very silly,
He likes chasing cats,
He likes chewing toys and bones
And even our welcome mat.

Stuart MacLeod (9)
Aird Primary School, Isle of Lewis

My Dog

My dog is stupid, yet loveable,
Soft, cuddly and huggable,
She's black, white and fluffy
And she is a dog who is always scruffy.

My dog is five and very alive,
If she could she would eat a beehive,
She eats fish, grass, meat and fruit
And she has a collection of stolen loot.

We've had her since she was six weeks old
And handled her like a piece of gold,
She used to sit upon my knee,
She has never once had a flea.

She has a plastic bed,
In which to lay her head,
She has a brain the size of a pea,
But I don't care she's my Bonnie D.

Eilidh Dodd (11)
Aird Primary School, Isle of Lewis

Blue

Blue is the colour blue,
Blue is the sky that is so bright,
Blue is the sea splashing on the shore,
Blue is the cold,
Blue is the Rangers strip I wear,
Blue are the whales and dolphins swimming,
Blue is the moon at midnight,
Blue is the television,
Blue is the sky on the sunny days.

Johanna Macdonald (10)
Airidhantuim Primary School, Isle of Lewis

The Simpsons Poem

T he Simpsons is a jolly good show,
H erb Powell is Homer's half brother,
E veryone has catchphrases.

S impsons is the best cartoon,
I n the Simpsons house it is crazy,
M att Groening is the creator and the producer,
P inchy is Homer's pet lobster,
S anta's Little Helper is their dog,
O nly the Simpsons make me laugh,
N othing is as funny as Homer choking Bart,
S nowball 11 is their cat.

Murray Macdonald (10)
Airidhantuim Primary School, Isle of Lewis

Blue

Blue is the sea, rough and restless
Blue is the Rangers on top form
Blue is the summer sky with drifting clouds sailing by
Blue is intense cold and toes
Blue is Scotland the Brave
Saltire floating proudly in the breeze
Blue is the Argentinian team
Crespo, Messi and Saviola on fire with tactics, skills and goals!

Ian MacDonald (11)
Airidhantuim Primary School, Isle of Lewis

My Acrostic Poem

A lways playing football, the game that I love,
L unch is always the best time of the day,
E ggs, bacon, sausage and beans is my favourite for breakfast,
X -rays are boring, they just look at bones,
A pples are my favourite fruit - yummy!
N ectarines are my least favourite,
D ogs are nice, but not the best,
E arwigs are ugly, they just bite you and bite you,
R eached the end, now you know all about me.

Alexander Macdonald (9)
Airidhantuim Primary School, Isle of Lewis

The Beast

It might be under your bed right now,
Looking for fresh juicy blood,
Haunting the dark, dreary and damp streets,
Searching for a petrified victim,
Its frizzy hair spiked up,
Like it's been electrocuted,
Licking its lips like a cat about to pounce,
Big dark eyes as black as pearls,
Fangs as sharp as knives.

Micheil Smith (11)
Airidhantuim Primary School, Isle of Lewis

The River

The river is a snake,
Twisting and hissing,
Its forked-tongue turning both ways,
It swirls down to the end of the lake.

The river is a monster,
Dragging things deep down,
Its mouth devours lots of rubbish,
From city, village and town.

The river is a baby,
Crying, gurgling he will creep,
He likes to suck his thumb,
But he never falls asleep.

The river is a wanderer,
He wanders all day,
He splashes like mad,
Hates stuff falling in, so don't do it any day.

Beth Macleod (9)
Airidhantuim Primary School, Isle of Lewis

The Rocket

About to take-off,
So explosive and loud,
Everyone clapping and very proud.

The astronauts go straight into space,
Even though one forgot his suitcase.

As they get closer, the moon gets bigger,
But at the window, there's a strange figure.

As they get closer, the figure gets bigger,
As it breaks in and pulls the trigger,
Bang! Bang!

Ian Mackay (11)
Airidhantuim Primary School, Isle of Lewis

The Monster Under My Bed

The monster under my bed,
Scares me in the night,
He has a big head,
I'm scared when I turn off the light.

The monster under my bed,
I dream about him in my sleep,
He always has to be fed,
I hate it when I hear him creep.

Suddenly I wake up
And find it was just a dream,
It was a shadow from my cup,
After Mum calling the monster team!

Kayleigh Smith (10)
Airidhantuim Primary School, Isle of Lewis

The River

The river is a snake,
Slowly twisting and turning,
Swimming smooth and swift,
His forked tongue curling!

The river is a home,
Protecting the fish and its babies,
Marching like a guard through the water,
Walking elegantly like ladies!

The river is a crab,
Crawling through the sea,
Cutting through the nets,
Setting himself free!

Catriona Rennie (9)
Airidhantuim Primary School, Isle of Lewis

My Dad

My dad says I'm weird,
My dad says I'm a pest,
My dad says I'm wild,
My dad says I'm as wild as a bear beating a gorilla,
My dad says I'm the truck of his life,
My dad says I'm one of The Animaniacs on TV,
My dad says I'm a loony,
My dad says I'm an idiot,
My dad says I'm just like Blackie,
My dad says I'm really reckless,
My dad says I'm Bart Simpson.

My dad says I hate pizza (not true),
My dad says my room looks like a bomb has hit it,
My dad says he loves me,
My dad says that I don't have any friends,
My dad says that I'm stupid,
My dad says that I'm cheeky,
My dad says that I'm a brat,
My dad says that I'm a destructive madman.

My mum says - I'm just like my *dad!*

Sarah Urry (9)
Avoch Primary School, Avoch

Wrestling

You have to be strong to be a wrestler,
Like John Cena,
You have to have muscles like John Cena,
You have to be able to fight like John Cena,
You have to be able to punch like John Cena,
You have to charge like a bulldog,
You have to be able to throw like The Hulk.

Scott Rice (9)
Avoch Primary School, Avoch

Dinosaur

D id the dinosaurs roam the world?
I n the dinosaurs' world, the meat eating are kings,
N o dinosaurs as strong as the T-Rex,
O ut the way, we're the plant eating dinosaurs,
S cary, nothing can save you now,
A s big as a skyscraper,
U nable to attack the T-rex,
R umble goes the T-rex's belly,
I am going to eat you!

Callum Hoare (9)
Avoch Primary School, Avoch

Jessie!

My dog Jessie is very messy,
She scratches on doors and digs up kitchen floors,
She tries to catch her tail
And never seems to fail,
She is half lurcher and half collie,
Though she is very scruffy,
She runs very fast
And is always excited.

Hannah McLaughlin (10)
Avoch Primary School, Avoch

My Baby Cousin

L ittle, lovely, laughing, lying,
E ars small and smooth,
W ake up early, warm hands grabbing,
I ll indoors crying,
S kin smooth, soft as silk.

Laura Miller (10)
Avoch Primary School, Avoch

Dinosaurs

D inosaurs, dinosaurs, dinosaurs,
I n the ground,
N ot on land,
O n the Earth millions of years ago,
S tegosaurous and T-Rex were quite fierce
A nd
U p in the sky the Quelzalcouthus flew,
R aptors ate loads of meat,
S o be very afraid.

Calum Wylie (10)
Avoch Primary School, Avoch

The Monster

Huge as a skyscraper,
Pure, poisonous, purple,
Scales all over his body,
Arms snatching people,
Feet stamping and crashing,
Gobbling children,
Exceedingly fat like a sumo wrestler,
People screaming, terrified,
Sprinting as fast as lightning.

Calum Brindle (9)
Avoch Primary School, Avoch

My Monster

I'm Pete and I'm petrifyingly poor
And I've got a monster under the door,
It growled in the night
And it gave me a fright,
So I ran out into the moors.

Jack Beasley (10)
Avoch Primary School, Avoch

The Holidays

Holidays are happy, holidays are jolly,
Looking forward to going abroad,
Flying in a plane, high in the sky,
Have lots of ice cream, lots of fun,
Sunny days,
Not like home,
No school, no homework,
Sun scorching, shining in the sky.

Sarah Miller (10)
Avoch Primary School, Avoch

Hallowe'en

Hallowe'en is the time of terror,
When ghosts as white as snow stalk their prey,
Frightening zombies covered in black dust,
Chase terrified children through town,
Horrifying spirits rampage in the darkness,
The smell of dead bodies fills the air,
You don't want to mess with your ghosts and
Your ghoulies on Hallowe'en.

Jack Hasson (9)
Avoch Primary School, Avoch

Monster In My Cup Of Tea

Have you see the monster in my cup of tea?
The brutal animal frightens me,
It is as fierce as a dragon,
He is as big as a sumo wrestler,
For a tiny animal, he is too ferocious.

Jack Cartwright (9)
Avoch Primary School, Avoch

How To Get Rid Of A Monster Under Your Bed

Have you ever seen a monster under your bed
And got you so scared, you jumped out of the window?
Well try . . .
Whipping it on the back, until it is as red as blood,
If that doesn't work,
Jump on the bed, until your head hits the top of the roof,
If that doesn't work,
Get your mum to suck its guts out with a Hoover,
Until it is as flat as a flipper
And if that doesn't work,
There's only one thing for it -
Run!

Chris Kelly (10)
Avoch Primary School, Avoch

My Best Friend

O livia likes olives,
L ovely Livie likes loilies,
I mportant like the Queen,
V aluable as china,
I ntelligent obviously,
A s strong as a rock.

Kathryn Cooper (9)
Avoch Primary School, Avoch

My Cat Smudge

S oft as silk,
M arvels at playing,
U pset when someone stands on her tail,
D ainty delicate dancing,
G ood as gold,
E njoys climbing.

Rebecca Winton (9)
Avoch Primary School, Avoch

The Weather

The weather is so amazing,
The snow falls as light as a feather,
The thunder and lightning crash and bang,
The sun, it is bright as a light,
The rain, it is as soaking as the ocean,
The hail, it bounces as high as a bouncy ball,
The clouds calmly cover canyons and countrysides,
The wind is as strong as a wrestler,
A heatwave is as hot as fire,
So you see, the weather is amazing!

Ross MacIver (9)
Avoch Primary School, Avoch

My Pet Mindy

Mindy is really cute and furry,
Mindy is really funny and thin,
Mindy is so soft,
Mindy is so funny when she looks at a dog,
Mindy is cuddly and hyper,
Mindy likes to sleep a lot,
Mindy is a very good kitten.

Laura Gill (9)
Avoch Primary School, Avoch

Fire

Tongues of flame, licking the air,
Tiny sparks flying and glowing like fireflies,
Crackles and bangs and dancing light,
That everyone can see,
It's a fairly funny thing that something so scary,
Is also a wonderful comfort.

Cathel Robertson (10)
Avoch Primary School, Avoch

Sam

My name is Sam,
My friends call me 'Grizzly Bear'
With my fuzzy, frizzy hair,
I like to play,
The computer,
My favourite game is
Super Shooter,
I love to read comics,
My favourite one is Sonic,
I really annoy
My teacher,
By making sounds,
Like a hurt creature,
I love to eat sweets,
But I hate chewy meats,
My friends think I'm really cool,
Because I have a giant swimming pool.

Angus Todd (10)
Avoch Primary School, Avoch

Running

My hobby is to run,
I like it 'cause it's super fun,
I put my leg in front of the other
And at the side watching me is my mother,
When I run, I feel a tingle in my belly,
My brother's watching whilst eating jelly,
The people I'm against are very fast,
But I'm pretty sure I won't come last,
I'm coming in 3rd place
And trying to keep a brave face,
The race has finished and I came in 2nd place,
But it was a brilliant race.

Mhairi MacFarlane (9)
Avoch Primary School, Avoch

My Cats

My fluffy cat,
Just like a bat,
So black,
So fat,
But playful, as well,
He'll sit on the stairs,
If you don't watch out, you'll go flying down!

My other so grey,
So interesting,
So posh,
I bet you it has got some dosh.

It's night now,
I switch off my light
And say goodnight.

Rachel McLauchlan (9)
Avoch Primary School, Avoch

Football

I love football,
It's my best hobby,
I always play with my dad,
Until he gets mad,
My dream is to play for Liverpool,
But everyone is so mean,
The best player for Liverpool is Gerrard by far,
He drives my favourite car,
Football is so much fun,
My mum tells me to have lots of buns,
To keep me strong
And to keep me long,
So I can jump and header the ball.

Calvin MacLean (10)
Avoch Primary School, Avoch

My Cuddly Hamster

My hamster is nice and fluffy, she is a chocolate brown,
She always sniffs out food when she is in her bed,
For now I must go and play with her,
For she must be a little bored
And now she is out of her cage and curling in my hand,
Now she's happy playing with me and also glad she's out,
For she's running around and chewing at the carpet,
I tell her, 'No that's bad!'
And now she's climbing the cage,
For she's tired from that night
And now she's in her cage and runs to her bed
And I whisper after her, 'Goodnight, I'll see you a different night!'

Megan Oag (9)
Avoch Primary School, Avoch

My Brother

My brother is Grim Reaper, every time he comes,
he tickles me deeper,
My brother gives me games, games all around,
My brother is the best,
My brother is my only brother,
It's not likely I will have another brother,
I wish my brother lived with us, but that is not true.
My brother.

Sandy Morrison (9)
Avoch Primary School, Avoch

Space

The flaming hot sun floats in the sparkling sky in space,
There are dark and bright stars covering its face,
Going up to space is a very nice place,
But it takes a long time to take-off from its base.

Andrew Reid (9)
Avoch Primary School, Avoch

Space

I went up to space, up to space I went,
I saw a dark star, I saw a bright star,
I saw a shooting star shooting
Big bright sun,
Sparkling in the dark night sky,
I saw a bright planet surrounded in bright stars,
I crossed a sparkling satellite,
Across from the Milky Way,
A star was dying,
Well I was flying,
Across from the big blue Neptune,
There was a little moon,
It covered no way near a balloon,
I don't, won't go,
There it must be pretty cold,
If we go over to Venus,
Let's go on the sand,
It will be like three sun beds,
I will need a hand with it if we go to Mars,
We will find lots of Mars bars,
If we go to the moon,
We could live on cheese,
If we go to Saturn we will find nothing but gold.

Struan Mackenzie (9)
Avoch Primary School, Avoch

The Ocean

The ocean has an amazing shine,
The ocean has a great amount of water,
I love the sweet, salty sound of the ocean,
The shiny dolphins dazzle in the ocean,
I see lots of fish,
I'd love to have a fish.

Calum Sutherland (10)
Avoch Primary School, Avoch

Monkeys!

Monkeys are mad,
They're as furry as moss,
They're extremely active
And never get lost,
They messily munch at meals,
There are all different kinds of monkeys,
Like gorillas and chimpanzees
And they all live together in an enormous tree,
Oh how I love these cheeky monkeys.

Sarah-Jayne MacNaughton (9)
Avoch Primary School, Avoch

Swimming Club

I love my swimming club,
Under I go *glub, glub, glub,*
When I dive,
I feel alive,
My good head coach,
Looks like a cockroach,
My favourite stroke is butterfly,
Every time I reach the sky,
I love swimming.

Olivia Philips (10)
Avoch Primary School, Avoch

The Ocean

The ocean is so steady, so calm and so gentle,
It can be rough and stormy but it's normally quite fine,
The floor of it is fine, but is quite divine,
In the floor of the ocean lives some fish
That can make a lovely fishy dish,
The ocean is so steady, so calm and so gentle.

Robert Norval (9)
Avoch Primary School, Avoch

Our Solar System

Saturn, Jupiter and Uranus,
All have rings,
Oh no! Not Mars, Earth or Venus they have no rings.

Mercury, oh so small,
So hot,
Poor little dot.

Not Neptune, so different,
Freezing,
Dark,
So far,
Not as small as a star.

Jupiter,
Lovely colours,
Metallic brown and blue,
No one has a bit of a clue,
Lovely moons glow though.

Earth,
One moon,
Earth is a kind of multicoloured balloon,
One sun,
We all have fun.

All our planets and more,
So pretty,
So fun,
Surrounding the sun.

Olivia Gubbins (9)
Avoch Primary School, Avoch

Bullying

Rushing to get home so they don't catch me,
Coming after me like a bird trying to catch its prey,
Haunting you every second of the day,
Hiding in the corner of the world like a spider,
Dull thoughts running through my head,
Or am I just paranoid?
They glare at you like a pack of wolves,
It feels like a black cloud over my head,
What word would you use to describe these feelings?
Well I would call it *bullying!*

Craig McIntosh (11)
Avoch Primary School, Avoch

The Past River

I am the river that saw the last dinosaur before it died,
I'm the river into which the Picts threw clay pots,
spear heads and iron for gifts,
I am the river where the smelly Celts washed their blue skin,
I'm the river where the bloodthirsty Vikings washed their swords
And threw the bodies of the ones they killed into me
And rowed that big longboat in my mouth,
I am the river with all the salmon that Queen Victoria aimed to get,
a lot of salmon.

Lewis MacNamara (10)
Avoch Primary School, Avoch

My Dog

My dog is so funny because she plays football
To have some fun,
My dog is so cool, she does what she wants,
My dog is fluffy as could be,
My dog is so fast, I couldn't even catch her,
My dog's teeth are sharp as broken glass.

Zoe Anderson (9)
Avoch Primary School, Avoch

All Seasons

Spring is lovely and warm,
Flowers grow like tulips and daisies,
The sky is a bright, bright blue,
Also the grass is greeny too,
In spring Easter is,
Lots of eggs, real eggs and chocolate,
We all shout hooray,
As we stuff our faces with chocolate.

Summer is sunny and hot,
Birds fly and sing a nice song,
As we go on holiday to an even hotter place,
We say bye bye to our home and
Go to Spain or Portugal,
The sun smiles as we go away,
When we get there our ice cream melts right away.

Autumn is cold and dark,
The leaves fall off trees,
They change colour from yellow, red then brown,
Autumn is my birthday,
The 8th of September,
You will not get red noses or cheeks,
I go outside and watch the lovely sky.

Winter is cold and icy,
The leaves have fallen off the trees,
You can feel a cold breeze,
Snow lies on the ground,
Icicles hang from the drain,
Written in the snow is 'Have a nice day,'
The start of a new year tomorrow, I can't wait!

Tanisha Duncan-Hood (9)
Avoch Primary School, Avoch

My Dog Scooby

My friendly puppy,
Just like a bunny,
So chocolate,
So funny
And looks so yummy,
As fast as a bird can be!

My puppy is so cute and small,
As can be!
He comes when he is called and
Does what he is told!

He has a little house that
Looks so nice
And he has a little door,
That is flat, flat, flat!

He likes scaring pheasants
And he loves the water and
Barks like mad and looks so sad
When you leave him at home!

Megan Grigor (9)
Avoch Primary School, Avoch

Big River

River, river, from you we drink,
River, river, to you we weep,
River, river, we collect your fossils,
River, river, you saw the last dinosaurs,
River, river, how old are you?
River, river, why do you cry?
River, river, I hope you never die.

Alexander McClymont (10)
Avoch Primary School, Avoch

Hallowe'en

Dark, dark, night smash of the thunder on the ground,
Ghosts and ghouls go by the haunted house,
Kids dress up as vampires, witches, ghosts, ghouls and gargoyles,
Bats at night fly past the gigantic moon,
Werewolves howl on the high, high hilltops at midnight,
Deep in the forest the wind blows through the tall, tall trees,
Crows screech in the night sky.

Fraser Williams (9)
Avoch Primary School, Avoch

Animals

Giraffe necks are long enough to reach the top of a tree,
It would be a miracle to find a gorilla in my back garden,
I would love to ride on a tiger,
It would be great to swim with crocs,
I would love to climb a tree with a bear,
It would be great to fly with birds,
Animals are great things, cute and fluffy, scary and scaly.

Tommy Ross Holm (9)
Avoch Primary School, Avoch

Ocean

The dazzling ocean glows,
As the sea winds blow
And the fresh and saltwater flows,
As the sea fish come and go
And the amazing dolphins do a fantastic little show,
As the tide is so low
And the whale blows the water out of its hole.

Donna MacNally (9)
Avoch Primary School, Avoch

Space

The shooting stars fly up to Mars,
For people say that Mars is made of marzipan,
The big bright sun,
Sees the flashing rockets go by
And the lava sun smiles and says hi,
The small tiny Mercury is as hot
As anything can be,
Neptune is as cold as in hospital,
When you have froze,
The shooting stars say bye to Mars,
As they fly to Jupiter,
With the five rocky moons,
They smile with a baboon face,
Venus is warm and cosy for its name is the
Bright, yellow sparkling Venus.

Ailsa Anderson-Todd (8)
Avoch Primary School, Avoch

My Poem About A River

As I walk down the river bank,
I am the river that rushes by,
I am the river that Bonnie Prince Charles
Washed his face in, this river,
I am the river that's winding to and fro,
I am the river that's tumbling down a waterfall,
I am the river that's turning right and left,
I am the river that's swirling round and round,
This is how it ends, well, a river never ends so a
poem never ends . . .

Nicola Hyslop (10)
Avoch Primary School, Avoch

Prehistoric River

I am the oldest river,
I will lift you off your feet,
I will make you shiver,
I am a river that flows over the rapids,
I have seen the Picts,
Building their house beside me,
Watching their luminous faces,
I have seen the Vikings,
Taking over Britain,
Killing off the Picts,
I saw Bonnie Prince Charlie climbing out of his boat,
Running from the English,
I have seen Queen Victoria fishing for salmon in my mouth,
I am a river that still lives today.

John Clarke (10)
Avoch Primary School, Avoch

Splash

I have been here since the Ice Age,
The Celts put iron in me for the gods,
The Picts washed their blue faces in me,
People set some fires to keep warm,
I have been drank from,
Some people swam in me,
My currents are dangerous,
From hundreds of years ago,
The salmon still leap high,
The sun is still high,
But I shall have to say goodbye,
The iron and goods are still in me.

Jake Anderson (10)
Avoch Primary School, Avoch

Rivers

I am the river Black Water that saw the last dinosaur,
I am the river Black Water that the Celts sacrificed
their nails, axes and spears too,
I am the river Black Water that the Picts washed their blue skin in,
I am the river Black Water that the Vikings paddled
their long boats in,
I am the river Black Water that Bonnie Prince Charlie's bones lie in,
I am the river Black Water that Queen Victoria caught her
first salmon in,
I am the river Black Water that started as a trickle.

Malcolm Wilson (10)
Avoch Primary School, Avoch

River!

I am the river where the dinosaurs took their last drink,
I am the river of melted ice from the Ice Age,
I am the river of the cavemen's basin where they washed away,
I am the river where Queen Victoria painted my water streaming,
I am the river where the shipmen rowed in their boats,
I am the river with sparkling water where the children come to play,
I am the river where people come to fish for fresh Scottish salmon.

Maddie Skinner (10)
Avoch Primary School, Avoch

Rivers

A mammoth's footprint lies in my mouth,
At the bottom of me some spears lie thanks to Stone Age men,
Picts washed their faces in me,
Vikings beached in my harbour,
Edward's army took a dip in me,
Royal Victoria fished for my fish,
Today I am stronger than ever.

Spike Setch (10)
Avoch Primary School, Avoch

In The River, The Mighty River

I am in a boat on the mighty river,
I start at a stream and come out at the mouth,
I like to think that ancient creatures swam the river
And Vikings swished downstream in longboats,
Kings and queens washed their faces and paddled in the shallows,
But now all the leftovers of that lovely life are fossils in the river,
The river flows at 100mph and the rapids splash against the banks
So I am in the boat on this mighty river.

Aidan Hersee (10)
Avoch Primary School, Avoch

I Am The River!

I am the river where the dinosaurs drank,
I am the river where the cavemen washed,
I am the river where the Vikings rowed their boats,
I am the river that's been here for centuries,
I am the river that Bonnie Prince Charlie walked past,
I am the river that Queen Victoria drew,
I am the river that children paddle in,
I am the river where families go to feed the ducks.

Michelle Reid (10)
Avoch Primary School, Avoch

One River

One river was flowing with dinosaurs' bones in,
One river was winding round in the Roman times,
One river was tumbling and thundering in the Ice Age,
One river was stood in by Queen Victoria decades ago,
One river was full of salmon when King Edward fished
some out for his tea,
One river is beside my house and it runs through my toes,
when I stand in it.

Georgina Cornes (10)
Avoch Primary School, Avoch

River!

I am a river of many ages,
I am the river that saw the last and first dinosaur,
I got things from the Celts to be blessed by the water gods,
I am the river that saw Picts painting themselves blue,
I am the river that saw Vikings drinking my water,
I am the river that saw Queen Victoria fishing for salmon,
I am the river that saw little kids playing on the banks,
I am the river that saw Queen Elizabeth eating on my banks,
I am the river that saw mostly everything but now I am
slowly going away.

Gillian Matheson (10)
Avoch Primary School, Avoch

The River

I am a river with rotten bones in it and smelly ones in it too,
I am a river where cavemen got their water and fish from,
I am a river with Vikings' weapons in,
I am a river with the Celts throwing spears in the river at gods,
I am a river with the Picts washing and drinking out of me,
I am a river with Queen Victoria fishing for my salmon,
I am a river that still lives now.

Connor David Johnston (10)
Avoch Primary School, Avoch

The Wonderful River

River, river, twists and turns,
River, river, swish and swirl,
River, river, rushing rapidly,
River, river, gushing water,
River, river, fossils in you,
River, river, flowing gently on a summer's morning.

Ceitidh Macdonald (10)
Avoch Primary School, Avoch

River

I am the river that saw the last dinosaur drink its fill,
I am the river that watched the Ice Age from start to end,
I am the river that has goods from the Celts rusting away in me,
I am the river that the Picts with their blue faces drank
and washed from.

I am the river the Vikings sailed up and down in,
I am the river that Queen Victoria painted,
I am the river that lots of ships first sailed on,
I am the river that you paddle in now.

Bethany Reid (10)
Avoch Primary School, Avoch

The River

I am the river that the dinosaurs drank
And the salmon run through my fingers,
I am swishing and swashing
And splishing and sploshing,
I am the river that the Picts had their water from,
The bones hitting off my toes,
I am the river that saw all the famous people swimming,
The mackerel are going into my ears,
The school children are putting their rubbish in me,
I may as well not be here.

Stefanie Skinner (10)
Avoch Primary School, Avoch

Friends To Machines

Martin is like a monster truck, he is tall and strong.

Liam is like a police car, he has lots of sirens.

Gus is like a Ferrari, he is fast, skilled and tough.

I am a Range Rover, big, sturdy and rough.

Cameron Mackenzie (11)
Avoch Primary School, Avoch

The River That Flows Past My House

I started as a trickle,
With iron where Vikings washed their spears,
Celts have dropped nails, axes into my water,
Queen Victoria came and sailed on me once or twice,
The streaming water flows through the valley,
Once they built a bridge across me,
Once a bridge fell into me,
Swirling and gushing I go,
William Wallace and Robert the Bruce walked across me in the war,
Thundering and tumbling I go,
Cattle drovers with cows and sheep went past,
I have been here for millennia,
They did ship building on me,
I hope I'll be here for ages more.

Jessica Hasson (11)
Avoch Primary School, Avoch

The River

The river where dinosaurs roamed wild and free,
The river where Picts hunted duck,
The river where salmon first came to live,
The wonderful river of Scotland.

The river where Vikings clashed their swords,
The river where fossils were first discovered,
The river where Queen Victoria drank from,
The historic river of Scotland.

The river your grandma played in as a girl,
The river that holds the secret to history,
The river I play and splash about in,
The fantastic river of Scotland.

Bethany Fea (10)
Avoch Primary School, Avoch

Bullying

I feel so alone,
So isolated,
They are not here . . . but I hear their laughs.

It's paranoia that I feel,
Life for me is grey, dull and sad.

They're behind every corner,
Behind every door, I feel so threatened,
I'm a victim, a sad and lonely victim,
I wish they'd leave me alone,
If I tell the teachers, they'll hurt me more,
I don't know what to do,
I'm a mouse trapped by cats,
I'm haunted by them, I don't know what to do,
I'm frightened of their shadows,
It doesn't feel good.

Martin McKenzie (11)
Avoch Primary School, Avoch

The Little Looking River

I'm the river that started as a trickle when
The melted water found a crack in a rock.
I have seen the world passing by, the Ice Age
To right this minute,
The Celts threw nails, axes and spears
To worship the water gods,
The Picts washed their blue bodies here,
Queen Victoria got some salmon here and right
This minute a fisherman is sitting on a rock,
Fishing in me!

Eleanor Leggatt (10)
Avoch Primary School, Avoch

The Buzzing Bee

Whizz! Whizz! Whizz! The buzzing bumblebee goes past my window,
Gleaming and shining like a dish out of the dish water,
The bumblebee looks at my nose squished on the
window like a pancake,
The bumblebee raced like a big blue Ferrari towards my window,
Splat! It hit the window like a train coming to a halt,
The bumblebee lay on the ground, like a dog getting its belly rubbed,
A loud buzz is heard like a jumbo jet,
It is the queen bee,
The queen bee flies over to the small bee
And touches it with its soft furry nose,
The small bee got up from the ground,
With more strength than it had ever had before,
The small bee fluttered off into the blue sky with strong shiny wings.

Kyle MacLeod (11)
Avoch Primary School, Avoch

The River That My Ancestors Drank Out Of!

I am the river that saw the last dinosaurs drink,
I am the river that lasted the Ice Age and that saw the first cavemen,
I am the river that saw the Picts making spears and swords,
I am the river that the Celts worshipped,
I am the river that the Vikings' longboats went in and out of,
I am the river that the cavalry rode past,
I am the river that Queen Victoria fished for salmon in,
I am the river that boats race in,
I am the river that has been flowing for years and years
And I am still flowing today.

Joe Hersee (10)
Avoch Primary School, Avoch

Naughty Nathan

Baking is as boring as watching paint dry,
If only I had something better to do,
Oh why, oh why, oh why.

I think and I grab the flour from
Miss Penny's hand,
This idea is the best idea I know I've ever had.

Up the stairs I go, heading for the staffroom,
Hearing my teacher's voice miles and miles behind me.

Just as I expected, the staffroom empty as usual,
Now I have plenty of time fixing the flour on top of the door
And waiting for the excitement.

I hear my teacher's footsteps and know that this will work,
I also know where the flour belongs -
Bang! 'Nathan!'
On the teacher's head.

Matilda Walker (11)
Avoch Primary School, Avoch

My River

I am a river that saw the last dinosaur drink its last drink,
I am a river that saw the Ice Age melt and finish,
I am a river that Celts got killed in,
I am a river that once had Picts washing their blue skin in me,
I am a river that the Vikings put iron in for their gods,
I am a river that saw Queen Victoria painting me when
she came to Scotland,
I am a river that saw the ship-building men,
I am a river that little children paddle in now.

Emma Matheson (10)
Avoch Primary School, Avoch

Raffin

Raffin is like a bouncy bunny,
A handful inside and out,
Her eyes are brown not crystal clear
And she's always out and about,
Her fur is white and patchy-brown,
She loves it when friends are around,
But when it's cold, she stays indoors,
Without a peep or a sound,
She never barks at strangers,
She never barks at me,
The only time she would ever bark,
Is if she was up a tree,
Her ears are brown and fluffy,
Her paws are small and grey,
She's always up to something
And she always wants to play
And we are friends,
Very good friends,
I hope her life never comes to an end!

Rachel McIlhenny (11)
Avoch Primary School, Avoch

Scotland

S cotland's famous flower is called the thistle,
C ome and see Scotland's entertainers, Katie Morag and
Oor Wullie,
O ver the hills and far away, lie the Highlands and Islands,
T umbling, crumbling, big far, rumbling, falling down castles
all over the place,
L ovely long lochs stream through and round Scotland,
A mazing animals lie in Scotland, pheasants, dolphins and deer,
N aughty Nessie has lived in Loch Ness, for over 300 years!
D iving dolphins, intelligent things, dipping and diving all
over the place.

Isla Jane Mackay (8)
Avoch Primary School, Avoch

Laughter

Laughter feels like the sun's rays,
Warm on your back,
Laughter feels like sand in your toes,
Leaving a footprint track.

Laughter smells like roses in bloom,
With bees buzzing above the ground,
Laughter smells like hot cross buns,
That are warm, plump and round.

Laughter tastes like honey,
Sweet and fresh from beehives,
Laughter tastes like candyfloss,
Brightening up our lives.

Laughter looks like sparkling jewels,
All in a chest,
Laughter looks like the sun on the sea,
Which really is the best.

Laughter sounds like party poppers,
With streamers flying about,
Laughter sounds like dolphins,
A talk that's almost a shout.

Halla Bell-Higgs (11)
Avoch Primary School, Avoch

Scotland

S cotland has spiky thistles and windy weather,
C rumbling castles and hairy haggis,
O or Wullie lives in the massive mountains,
T owering trees cover the misty moors,
L ovely lochs roam the land
A nd huge hills conquer it,
N ever-ending splendid sights,
D o you approve of everlasting Scotland?

Ben Beasley (7)
Avoch Primary School, Avoch

Scotland

S cotland's Loch Ness is wet and slimy,
C rumbling castles on top of green hills,
O or Wullie and The Broons are two Scottish cartoons,
T histles are spiky in the dark forest at night,
L ittle fluffy animals like to run and play all day,
A ll the rocky mountains reach up high,
N essie in the deep big Loch Ness,
D olphins are swooping up and down on the wavy sea.

Amy Beattie (8)
Avoch Primary School, Avoch

Scotland

S cotland flags flying everywhere,
C rumbly castles up the huge hills,
O or Wullie playing in Dundee,
T he capital of Scotland is Edinburgh,
L ots of squirrels run up the tall trees,
A ll the towering trees in the forests are lovely,
N essie is the monster who lives in Loch Ness,
D olphins diving and flipping in Scottish seas.

Keira Jack Macleod (8)
Avoch Primary School, Avoch

Scotland

S piky thistles in the grass,
C ool ceilidhs in the highlands,
O tters come up to the sandy shore,
T artans are on leather kilts,
L ovely lochs and lighthouses,
A mazing massive mountains and the hills and glens,
N essie the Loch Ness monster,
D iving dolphins at the seaside.

Cameron Young (8)
Avoch Primary School, Avoch

Scotland

S cottish saltire in our flag,
C ool ceilidhs are very common,
O or Wullie and The Broons are so brilliant,
T artans are very colourful,
L arge lovely Loch Ness monster,
A mazingly monstrous mountains,
N oisy bagpipes fill the air,
D ucks can fill every village, town and city.

Lorcan Downing-James (8)
Avoch Primary School, Avoch

Scotland

S cotland is lovely,
C olourful tartan,
O or Wullie and The Broons,
T rees have lots of squirrels,
L ovely huge hills,
A nimals in the forests,
N ice Nessie lives in Loch Ness,
D on't you think Scotland is cool?

Duncan Burns (8)
Avoch Primary School, Avoch

Scotland

S cotland has huge hills,
C old, dark, crumbly castles,
O tters like to fish a lot,
T he spiky thistle grows wild,
L ovely views over the great glens
A nd all the feathery pheasants flutter,
N ess is a beautiful monster,
D olphins are diving and ducking in the sea.

Brogan Fuerst (9)
Avoch Primary School, Avoch

Scotland

S ee Scotland and its huge hills,
C ool cottages by the beautiful seashores,
O ver stormy seas find our beautiful
T owering Ben Nevis in the dark forests,
L ovely lochs full of flipping fish,
A monster might be in Loch Ness,
N ice leisure in the thick forests,
D iving dolphins and flipping fish in the stormy seas.

Lewis Franklin (8)
Avoch Primary School, Avoch

Scotland

S cotland the brave,
C rumbly castle and flying fish,
O or Wullie and The Broons,
T rees and forests with lots of red squirrels,
L ovely lochs and great glens,
A mazing animals and hairy haggis,
N oisy bagpipes playing at cool ceilidhs,
D iving dolphins and flipping fish in the stormy seas.

Isatou Jallow (8)
Avoch Primary School, Avoch

Scotland

S cotland is famous for golf,
C ool ceilidhs - dancing,
O or Wullie and The Broons you will find here,
T owering Ben Nevis in the great glen,
L ovely lighthouses along our beaches,
A ll the food is delicious in Scotland,
N essie lives in the bottom of the loch,
D ucks fill the ponds of Scotland.

Drew Mann (8)
Avoch Primary School, Avoch

Scotland

S cotland is wonderful,
C rumbly castles beside lovely lochs,
O ver the hills flies the eagle,
T artan is made to make colourful kilts,
L ovely lighthouses on the beautiful beaches,
A nimals are hiding in the great glen,
N oisy bagpipes in the tall church,
D andelions and thistles grow in the wild grass.

Becki Kirkwood (8)
Avoch Primary School, Avoch

Scotland

S cotland has big hills and mountains,
C ome and see the jumping dolphins flipping and fishing,
O ver the storming sea, you can find beautiful islands,
T owering Ben Nevis in the great glen,
L ovely loch where Nessie lives,
A monster might be in the Loch Ness,
N ice green trees in the forest,
D on't you think Scotland is spectacular.

Ben Kelly (8)
Avoch Primary School, Avoch

Scotland

S cotland is famous for football,
C rumbly castles and huge hills,
O or Wullie playing with his mates,
T here are lots of tall trees in Scotland,
L ots of squirrels running in the woods,
A lways fish by the sandy shores,
N essie lying in his loch,
D iving dolphins in the sparkling sea.

Craig MacNamara (8)
Avoch Primary School, Avoch

Scotland

S cotland has amazing animals,
C ool ceilidhs and fun castles,
O or Wullie and Broons are really funny,
T alking birds really high in the lowered trees,
L ovely trees and hills,
A poet called Robert Burns lived here,
N oisy birds soar in the sky,
D o you want to visit Scotland?

Michael Williamson (8)
Avoch Primary School, Avoch

Scotland

S cotland's flag is saltire,
C rumbly castles and lovely lochs,
O n the hills eagles fly,
T histles are spiky and cool,
L och Ness is so lovely and great glens,
A nimals on the big Ben Nevis,
N ice Nessie is big and beautiful,
D olphins are diving in big lochs.

Ross Munro (9)
Avoch Primary School, Avoch

Scotland

S cotland is beautiful and wonderful,
C ome and see the soft snow,
O h please come see us, you can see diving dolphins,
T he seaside is lovely,
L ovely mountains you can see,
A monster might be in the lochs,
N ever dive in the lochs,
D o come, please.

Adam Millington Bailey (8)
Avoch Primary School, Avoch

Like A Tree

Trees are actually quite intelligent,
They are friendly and much liked,
Like a tree is a teddy bear,
You can talk to them,
About anything and they listen,
Like a tree is life,
Always changed every time,
You look back at it,
Like a tree is school,
Lots of different pupils,
All with different shapes, sizes
And personalities,
Like a tree is a book,
With different chapters,
Throughout it
And this is where I finish
My poem,
Not too long,
Not too short,
But just right I would say,
To keep your mind wondering,
About what else trees are like!

Jessica Leggatt (11)
Avoch Primary School, Avoch

Scotland

S cotland is a lovely land,
C ool as can be,
O or Wullie is a great cartoon,
T here's lots of tall trees in the hills,
L ovely views and birds of prey,
A lways wet, wild and windy,
N oisy music and bagpipes,
D iving dolphins are living in our waters.

Mhairi Mackay (8)
Avoch Primary School, Avoch

Bullying

Sitting alone,
All alone,
Looking left and right,
Checking if they are there,
Checking if they are watching me,
Like a mouse in a mouse hole,
Checking for cats,
Fierce cats,
And I'm the victim,
Me all alone, by myself.
The world around me is dull and grey,
I feel threatened,
Even though there's nothing there,
Nothing, no one,
I want to disappear,
Fade away, leave the world,
Forever,
My face is pale,
Pale as a ghost,
I may be fine today,
But will they be back tomorrow?

Ellis Mackenzie (11)
Avoch Primary School, Avoch

Scotland

S cotland is famous for great golf,
C rumbly castles on the hills,
O tters on top of rocks in the rivers,
T he land is beautiful,
L ovely lighthouses,
A ll the food is very delicious,
N essie lives in the Loch Ness,
D o come to Scotland.

Thomas Hardie (9)
Avoch Primary School, Avoch

My Family Tree!

Welcome to my family tree . . .

Moaning Mum
Mum is as moany as a kitten is cute,
Mum is a ghost
Moaning through a hallway!

Daft Dad
Dad is as daft as a blind dog
Bashing into things,
Dad is a clown,
Trying to be funny but
Not succeeding.

Silly Sister
Sister is as silly as a clown
In a circus,
Sister is a monkey,
That is trying to find her banana!

Boring Brother
Brother is as boring as a
Book on politics,
Brother is a lecture
On how cheese is made.

Eilidh Murray (11)
Avoch Primary School, Avoch

Bullying

Run like the wind, run . . . run,
The lion is ready to pounce,
Threatened by a glare,
Chased like an insect,
Your confidence broken like a twig,
Cornered by a slippery little snake,
Chased by bad luck itself,
Waiting for the golden age and peace.

Lewis Miller (11)
Avoch Primary School, Avoch

Kayaking To Squidgy Bay

Kayaking can give you lots of feelings,
Happy, tired, relaxed,
This poem is about things I love,
Sun, kayaking, Dad,
We luckily had a perfect day,
Breezy, clear, sunny.

Setting off and breaking free,
Rocks, waves, wind,
Passing rocks and becoming calm,
Glistening sea, sky,
Breeze guiding us, no need to paddle,
Trees, swaying, lightly.

Finally at our destination,
Pleased, proud, happy,
Eating apricots, healthy all the way,
Paradise, yum-yum,
Watch out for animals,
There could be a few,
Seals, birds, fish.

The challenge is only finished when we get home,
But let's . . . stay . . . for now!

Abigail Sked (11)
Avoch Primary School, Avoch

Scotland

S cotland has hills and lovely lighthouses,
C rumbling castles and lovely glens, they are lovely too,
O tters came for holiday for fishing and walk but some
came to catch Nessie,
T owering Nevis rumbles the sky, rivers rush to the sea,
L ovely lochs, one is famous for what lurks below,
A mazing cool ceilidhs dancing to and fro,
N othing is better than having walks in the countryside,
D olphins flipping in the sea, in the windy weather.

Ryan Bremner (9)
Avoch Primary School, Avoch

Life As A Westie

I am a Westie and my fleece is as white as snow,
I always like to bite my feet,
I hate it when I get blown in the face
And I love my toys too,
I cannot wait until dinner time,
Because I get my food,
I have got a big appetite,
So don't give me a little bite,
I love food as much as you,
But remember after dinner time,
I want my walk or I will bark forever,
After my walk do not take me straight in
Because I like to protect my fence,
After that I will go to bed.

Up I get ready to go outside.

I am outside and I'm waiting very noisily to get in,
My dad is standing in front of me,
Shouting my name so I go in and sleep on my bed.

Christopher Dickson (11)
Avoch Primary School, Avoch

What Are Friends?

Friends are people you share secrets with,
They are people you run to when you've had the worst day on Earth,
They come in many different sizes,
Some may be as fast as a speedboat or as slow as a snail,
It does not matter for they are your friend,
Friends are people you have fun with,
They are people you do fun things with,
You may just stay in or go out shopping or play football,
One thing you need to know is this -
Keep them close!
For if you don't, you may lose them!

Lucy Tease (11)
Avoch Primary School, Avoch

Friendship Group

Rebecca is a smiling heart,
She is allergic to a frown,
Emma is a shining sun,
She is always full of joy,
Katie is a public park,
New face every day,
Lauren is a cheeky monk,
Who's not afraid to say,
Rochelle is a drama queen,
She likes to express herself,
Laura is a laughing box,
Along with her smile,
Ellis is a perfect girl,
Her make-up, hair and nails,
Megan is a football champ,
I love her just for that,
Laura is a shy little chick,
With her sweet, soft voice,
Emma is a sparkling star,
Always shining with her smile
And altogether - we happen to make the perfect friends.

Rachelle McAllilster (11)
Avoch Primary School, Avoch

Bullying

I feel alone,
Worried if they come,
Feeling so dull,
I feel as if I'm surrounded,
Hoping they don't have weapons,
Needing my friends here,
Feeling like a fox caught by shooters,
I'm feeling so threatened,
Is this ever going to stop?
I hope they stop now.

Laura MacIver (11)
Avoch Primary School, Avoch

Bullying

They're coming,
What are they going to do?
Paranoid,
Laughing at me,
Alone,
Why did they have to pick me?
Black and grey all around,
Nobody for me,
I am the victim,
An island with nobody,
Intimidating me,
Like a fox getting chased,
Bloodthirsty dogs waiting for me,
Hiding away in the dark corners in my mind.

Rebecca Bremner (12)
Avoch Primary School, Avoch

Bullying

A bully can intimidate you,
A bully can threaten you,
A bully can victimise you,
A bully can come in a group,
A bully can make you feel as sick as a dog,
A bully will not stop,
One day the bully will make you pop,
A bully can make you feel alone,
But one day someone will change his tone,
'Sticks and stones may break your bones
But names will never harm me'.
That's not true,
Stop the bully before he stops you!

Ewan Catto (12)
Avoch Primary School, Avoch

Bullying

It's you, just you, on your own, but they're coming,
You are trapped on an island,
On your own, out of the world,
But you know they're coming,
Everything is grey or black and dull,
It's horrible,
You're threatened by people all around you,
You are the victim,
Paranoid that people are out to get you,
It feels like you are the timid little mouse
And they are the giants,
They intimidate you, until you're mad and shout,
But it doesn't scare them,
It's no use, you're the only one in this world
And it's not going to change.

Megan Jack (11)
Avoch Primary School, Avoch

Bullying

Gloomy,
Alone,
Isolated,
I feel as if I'm being watched,
I know they're coming,
I feel so dull,
I think I'm about to crack,
Inside I feel pain,
I try and not think about it,
But I can't help it,
I hear voices in my head that they're going to get me,
When will this stop?
That I don't know!

Emma Skinner (11)
Avoch Primary School, Avoch

Bullying

Here I sit on the wall,
Alone,
It's like a living nightmare,
It's quiet, although there's a whole crowd of
People around me,
I feel paranoid,
They're out to get me, I just know it!
I'm like a weak cornered mouse,
Facing a strong wailing cat,
There's a black cloud floating over me,
The world isn't colourful anymore,
It's dull, greys and blacks,
I want to just vanish,
I feel like a victim of war,
Ninety-nine to one,
I try to say to myself, it will be over soon,
I see things, horrible things,
I close my eyes, try to block them out,
My mind is playing tricks,
Please be over soon.

Lauren McKenzie (11)
Avoch Primary School, Avoch

Bullying

I feel like I'm on a deserted island,
They're like a lion ready to pounce,
I'm cornered, nowhere to escape,
I feel like I'm a mouse,
I'm paranoid expecting to turn and they will be there,
A dark cloud floats over my head
And will never disappear.

Gary Macleman (11)
Avoch Primary School, Avoch

Bullying

Bullying
It's something that no one likes,
You feel like you want to hide and never come out,
The bullies pass you and all you want to do is *run!*
You try to face them but when you try,
You can't do it,
It's like you're a mouse,
Being chased and teased,
You get home,
It is like the walls are closing in on you,
Just like when you are near the bullies,
You're relieved to get away,
At least until tomorrow,
Will it stop?
I hope it does.

Matthew Williams (11)
Avoch Primary School, Avoch

Bullying

Here I stand all alone,
No one with me,
I'm as quiet as a mouse,
I feel like they're here all the time,
Waiting to get me,
The world is in colour, I am in grey,
I feel the world is caving in on me,
As I stand in the corner, everything is still,
I feel lonely,
No friends to comfort me,
What can I do? Where can I go?
I can't cope anymore,
It's got to stop!
Why are they doing this?
Will it ever end?

Emma Paterson (11)
Avoch Primary School, Avoch

Bullying

Oh no!
There they are,
Like a lion running after its prey,
I finally stop,
Exhausted!
No one knows how I feel,
I am on my own,
I wipe my tear-stained face,
I feel intimidated, paranoid,
They threaten me,
I come out in a sweat,
I scream,
No one comes,
Why am I the victim?
They don't hit me,
Words are worse,
An itchy, sore cut but you can't scratch it,
Help!

Katie MacLeod (11)
Avoch Primary School, Avoch

My Teddy

He is small as a stone,
He has small brown eyes,
He is soft as a pillow,
He has a soft tail,
He has soft ears,
He has a small white nose,
He is twelve years old,
He lives in my bed,
He is very happy with his five friends,
He is called Doggy.

Ewan MacIver (11)
Avoch Primary School, Avoch

Bullying

Everybody crowds me,
Looking for a fight,
But only I know, that it's not going to happen,
I feel lonely,
I feel paranoid, threatened,
I'm on another island,
Sea surrounding,
I say they're victim fighters,
They're going to get me,
At any time,
I run,
They're coming,
I say,
My mind is getting eaten,
By them.

Katie Hardie (11)
Avoch Primary School, Avoch

My Best Friends

They are like a star,
Shining from all the rest,
They are like an angel,
Making us happy and welcome.

They are like a clock,
Never stops just keeps going,
They are like a flower,
Blooming up every day.

They are like a gift,
A part of your life,
They are my friends
And that matters.

Lynne Clark (11)
Avoch Primary School, Avoch

Friendship Safari

Cameron is an ape,
Big, strong and smart.

Gus is a porcupine,
Spiky-haired devil.

Martin is a giraffe,
Big, lanky, long legs.

Kyle is a cheetah,
Powerful and quick.

Niall is a meerkat,
Tough little cookie.

And who's like a monkey?
Cheeky young me!

Liam Alexander Mackenzie - (11)
Avoch Primary School, Avoch

Fear

Fear makes you scared,
Fear makes you terrified,
Fear freaks you out,
Fear is really scary,
Fear makes you think,
Fear really scares you,
Fear freaks you out,
Sometimes if you get attacked
By an animal you will fear it,
That could be a bat,
That could be a spider,
That could be a snake,
Fear freaks you out.

Andrew Lingard (11)
Avoch Primary School, Avoch

My Friends

Eilidh is as good as gold,
She hardly ever gets into trouble,
Abi is as speedy as a cheetah,
Maybe one day she could be in the Olympics,
Rachel is as fun as a dolphin,
She knows when you're upset and will come and cheer you up,
Lucy is as kind as a kitten,
She is a caring person and hardly ever lets you down,
Halla is encouraging as a manager of a football club,
Rachelle is as helpful as a bird,
She will always help you when she can
And she is always there for you,
Astrid is as talkative as a parrot,
Who never stops talking,
Matthew is as funny as a clown,
He is always clowning about,
These are my friends
And it will be a shame to lose them,
I don't know what I'll do without them.

Joanne Stewart (11)
Avoch Primary School, Avoch

Bullying

Alone,
The sound is being blocked out,
Everything is dull,
The world is spinning around me,
I am paranoid the whole time, even in bed,
They threaten me, they say they are going to kill me,
I am all alone, no one to help me,
It feels like I am trapped on an island without a flare,
I feel like my mind is playing tricks on me!

Daniel MacIver (11)
Avoch Primary School, Avoch

Feelings

Happiness is good, happiness is great,
You don't know when happiness comes into place.

Laughter is good, laughter is great,
You don't know when laughter comes into place.

Silence is good, silence is bad,
You don't know when silence comes into place.

Fear is scary, fear is bad,
You don't want fear to come in place!

Jamie Shand (11)
Avoch Primary School, Avoch

The Beautiful River

Beautiful river,
I am the river of life,
Clear as crystal.
I am the river that runs through the sea
And I am the river that Queen Victoria washed and drank from.
I am the river that was once in spate
And I am the river that Bonnie Prince Charlie once came to visit.
I am the river that started as a trickle.
I am the river full of gifts
And that's the lovely river of Scotland.

Laura Kelman (10)
Avoch Primary School, Avoch

Friends

Having friends is great
And never should you hate,
But I don't know who you are,
So I'd watch for the brightest star
And there you'll find a friend by far.

Gilliane Grainger (9)
Avoch Primary School, Avoch

Only Love

It's dark,
I miss everyone,
Here there is only 'Hate',
I'm scared,
I feel anger welling up inside me,
Why did they leave me?
Here in this desolate place?
It's so quiet,
If the sadness takes over me,
I'm sure I won't survive!
There is a light,
There has to be a light,
Where there is dark,
There is light!
It's getting bigger!
The light is getting bigger!
The darkness is going,
The light is taking over,
Happiness is coming,
People are having fun,
I'm not alone any more!
Sadness has dispersed,
Happiness is here,
The anger inside me has vanished!
No more 'Hate'
Only 'Love'.

Karoline Beigley (11)
Avoch Primary School, Avoch

Footy Rampage

Running to the pitch,
Fast as a cheetah.

To get moving like a bumblebee,
Always flying around.

Sitting on the grass like a teddy,
Sitting on your bed.

Panting like a tired dog,
Back from its walk.

Going home, waiting,
To get into my warm bed.

Angus Plowman (11)
Avoch Primary School, Avoch

Ocean Kennings

(In the style of 'Black Dot' by Libby Houston)

A myth maker
A dam breaker

A life taker
A noise creator

A creature holder
A land moulder

A boat sinker
A stone shrinker

A watery place
A shining grace

A surfer's dream
A sparkling gleam

A catalogue to make me . . . ocean.

Finlay Macpherson (11)
Balivanich Primary School, Isle of Benbecula

Horse Kennings

(In the style of 'Black Dot' by Libby Houston)

A carrot cruncher
An apple muncher

A Polo eater
A 'me' greeter

A rug wearer
A hay tearer

A water drinker
A fast blinker

A metal shoe
A friend for you

A catalogue to make me . . . horse.

Eilidh Muir (11)
Balivanich Primary School, Isle of Benbecula

Lobster Kennings

(In the style of 'Black Dot' by Libby Houston)

A minor dot
A tiny speck

A little fighter
A little nipper

A fierce hider
An eye shiner

A military soldier
A strong boulder
A catalogue to make me a lobster.

Donnie MacLean (11)
Balivanich Primary School, Isle of Benbecula

Puppy Kennings

(In the style of 'Black Dot' by Libby Houston)

A human licker
A stick picker

A shoe taker
A cat hater

A biscuit eater
A feet heater

A bone chewer
A cat shooer

A ball catcher
A family attacher

A catalogue to make me . . . puppy.

Meghan Davidson (11)
Balivanich Primary School, Isle of Benbecula

Newt Kennings

(In the style of 'Black Dot' by Libby Houston)

A black dot
A jelly tot

A frilly neck
A heron's peck

A minnow snapper
A land flapper

A crested champ
A vice clamp

A catalogue to make me . . . newt.

Calum Wells (11)
Balivanich Primary School, Isle of Benbecula

Horse Kennings

(In the style of 'Black Dot' by Libby Houston)

A metal shoe
A friend for you

A rug wearer
A hay tearer

A carriage puller
A field ruler

A noise maker
A ride taker

A carrot gobbler
A peach cobbler

A good filly
And never silly

A catalogue to make me . . . horse!

Lauren MacKay (11)
Balivanich Primary School, Isle of Benbecula

Sheep Kennings

(In the style of 'Black Dot' by Libby Houston)

A fluffy pillow
A woolly willow

A puffy cloud
White and round

A grass eater
A loud bleater

A fence jumper
A grass chomper

A catalogue to make me a . . . sheep.

James Hickey (12)
Balivanich Primary School, Isle of Benbecula

Happiness

Happiness is as blue as the sky,
It smells like roses,
It tastes like passion fruit,
It sounds like birds,
It feels like clouds,
It lives in the sky.

Kimberley Taylor (11)
Balivanich Primary School, Isle of Benbecula

A Poem About Pain

Pain's colour is red,
It smells like blood,
Pain tastes like burnt food,
It sounds like a storm
And it lives in a dark cave.

Allyssa Young (9)
Balivanich Primary School, Isle of Benbecula

Sadness Is . . .

Sadness is peach,
It smells like dusty old clothes,
It tastes like salty water
And sounds like a buzzy bee
And it lives in the dark corner
Of your heart.

Megan Mackay (10)
Balivanich Primary School, Isle of Benbecula

The Beauty Of Beauty

Beauty is purple and royal,
It looks like a butterfly about to take flight,
It smells like lovely lavender,
It sounds like classical music on the harp,
It takes its beauty sleep in a palace in France,
Looking out onto the Eiffel Tower
And that is the beauty of beauty.

Rebecca Hough (10)
Balivanich Primary School, Isle of Benbecula

Jubilation

Jubilation is a vivid pink,
Jubilation smells of white lilies,
Jubilation tastes like marshmallows,
Jubilation sounds like a soft humming,
Jubilation lives in a party popper.

Erin Warner (9)
Balivanich Primary School, Isle of Benbecula

Love Is Sweet

Love is sweet,
Love is red,
Love lives in a heart and sounds like romantic music,
It smells like sugar, it tastes like chocolate.

Cassandra Humphrey (10)
Balivanich Primary School, Isle of Benbecula

Happiness Is?

Happiness is multicoloured,
Smells like roses,
Tastes like strawberries,
Sounds kind,
Feels soft,
Lives in our hearts.

Kenneth Maclean (10)
Balivanich Primary School, Isle of Benbecula

Happiness

Happiness is pink and cheerful,
Happiness smells like roses,
Happiness tastes like sweet cakes,
Happiness sounds like soothing classical music,
Happiness lives in your heart.

Katie MacRury (10)
Balivanich Primary School, Isle of Benbecula

Respect

Respect is green,
Respect smells like chocolate muffins,
Respect tastes like toast,
Respect sounds like a cat purring,
Respect lives in the world.

Scott MacKay (10)
Balivanich Primary School, Isle of Benbecula

Respect

Respect is blue,
Smells like smoke,
Respect tastes like jam,
Sounds like drums,
It lives in your body.

Calum Jamie Murray (10)
Balivanich Primary School, Isle of Benbecula

Old Age

Old age is grey and wrinkly,
It smells like smoke,
Old age tastes like rotten milk,
It sounds like a dog that's never been fed,
Old age lives in an old people's home.

William Hickey (10)
Balivanich Primary School, Isle of Benbecula

Happiness Is . . .

The colour of happiness is bright and colourful,
The smell is sweet and not sour,
The taste is the sweetest sugar,
The sound is peaceful like a light wind,
It lives in your heart.

Cameron Reilly (11)
Balivanich Primary School, Isle of Benbecula

Pain Is . . .

Pain's colour is scarlet,
It smells of smoke,
It tastes like nettles,
It sounds like explosions,
Its pain's next-door neighbour.

Ruairidh Muncaster (10)
Balivanich Primary School, Isle of Benbecula

Hope

Hope is a very clear white,
It smells so sweet and relaxing,
It tastes like fresh fruit,
Sounds like words of encouragement
And lives in human hearts.

James Mackenzie (9)
Balivanich Primary School, Isle of Benbecula

Pain Is?

Pain is as black as coal.
Pain smells like rotten cheese.
Pain tastes like glitter.
Pain lives in the attic.
Pain sounds like wolves howling in the night.

John Allan Paul MacLeod (10)
Balivanich Primary School, Isle of Benbecula

Fear Poem

Fear is a great deep purple,
It smells . . . well . . . fearsome,
It tastes like bits of grit.

It sounds like a *howling gale.*
It lives in the heart of your heart.

Matthew Netherton (9)
Balivanich Primary School, Isle of Benbecula

Hope

Colour of pink,
Smell - sweet roses,
Taste - like sweets,
Sounds like beautiful music,
It lives in my heart.

Danielle Anderson (11)
Balivanich Primary School, Isle of Benbecula

Leopard Race

The racing car is like a leopard
Waiting to pounce
On its unsuspecting prey
Zoom! Faster than bolt of lightning
It hurtles from the start line
With a deafening roar
It hurtles along the racing track
Intent on winning
Outwitting its rivals
Its aim from the start.

Lewis Maclean (11)
Barvas Primary School, Isle of Lewis

The Sea

The sea is like wild horses
Horses to ride
Horses that frisk and frolic
They come in with the tide.

All day, all night
With flying manes
Kicking legs
They prance and pound
On the rocky shore.

But on calm days
When all is quiet and still
They frolic playfully
As they lap peacefully
Ready to rest.

Claire Paterson (10)
Barvas Primary School, Isle of Lewis

The Snowstorm

The snowstorm is a raging white tiger,
Savage and wild,
He rolls in the Arctic wilderness,
Biting bitterly and ripping his prey,
He cleans his dazzling fur every day.

Prowling and pouncing,
He always succeeds,
To catch his victim,
Ensnaring him in a thick white blanket.

But when the snowstorm settles
On calm quiet days,
He retreats to his den
Leaving a 'winter wonderland'.

Donald John Nicholson (11)
Barvas Primary School, Isle of Lewis

The Volcano

The volcano is like a tiger,
Sleeping for a while,
Waiting to come out and play,
Slowly, silently, secretly.
Waiting for the day
When he will erupt.

Hot-tempered, like a fire,
Blistering with outrage,
Choked-up with flame.
Then unexpectedly it murmurs, it mutters,
Then it *bellows* and *roars.*
Thick, puffy, grey clouds belch up
Towards the sky as it spits out its anger.

Infuriated it springs upright,
Red-hot like a poker,
Shaking and shivering
As it pounces its fury into the steamy air.

Anne-Marie Macleod (10)
Barvas Primary School, Isle of Lewis

Thunderstorm

The thunderstorm is a large elephant
Massive and careless,
Trumpets so loud and shaking the ground,
Grey as darkened fluffy clouds,
Rumbling as he walks.

Spitting water everywhere,
Hosing the jungle with his long, crinkly, grey trunk,
Stamping, stomping, destroying everything in its path.

Rumbling like an earthquake,
But slowly as day approaches
He quietly troops to the watering hole
To dip his rough trunk into the water.

Connor Morrison (9)
Barvas Primary School, Isle of Lewis

The Fast And The Furious

The super bike is like a shark
Darting and fierce
Leaping fast and furious
Accelerating, alert, menacing
Leaping from rest
Sparks spitting, sparks monstrous, menacing, flashing.

It streaks through the deep
Brisk as a leopard
Overpowering on its track
Tyres screaming on turns
Engine roaring, exhaust fumes pouring
Accelerating away past the chequered flag.

Flashing around the arena
Coming up to the last lap
Striving to overtake
One mad dash to the finish line
Hooray! Prize won at last!

Alasdair Morrison (10)
Barvas Primary School, Isle of Lewis

A Hawk

A hawk is a fast glider
Flying gracefully through the blue sky,
Searching for his quarry.
He finds his prey and swoops down for a meal,
He attacks, tearing voraciously.
Then off again,
Flying and zooming through the sky,
Beady eyes searching, searching,
Forever flapping wings furiously,
Hovering silently, circling around,
Until he flies satisfied to his craggy nest.

Graham Martin (9)
Barvas Primary School, Isle of Lewis

The Fighting Jet

A hawk is a fighter jet flying
Through the air fast and fragile.
He hunts on the rough moorland
With his pointed beak and sharp wings
Destroying everything.

He battles until he's finished
He's eager to eat anything in his path.

He's hungry for deconstruction
He will defend his territory
Fiercely cold-blooded.

When he sees his prey
He will plummet to the ground.
Then like a Concorde
Zooming he will soar.
Flying peacefully back to his nest
On the side of the cliff.

Mitchell Thompson (9)
Barvas Primary School, Isle of Lewis

The Earthquake

An earthquake is an unmanageable elephant
Massive and grey
He tramples down hefty trees all day
With his muscular body and mighty trunk
He pounds the ground into microscopic dust.

Every few minutes he takes a breath
And blows his trumpet for all to hear
Which puts an aching pain in your ears.

But on quiet days when the sky is dull and no one wanders out
He does not stampede, he does not shout
He lies down quiet and content
Not running out and about.

Hamish McTaggart (11)
Barvas Primary School, Isle of Lewis

The Volcano

A volcano is an unpredictable cobra,
Scaly and explosive.
He's starting to rumble today,
Many a time he's waited for this,
He's now beginning to *snarl, spit, hiss.*

Now it's seconds before the attack,
He is now arching up his back,
Here it comes, an almighty flame,
This is one beast you cannot tame.

This murderous creature needs more room,
It's now at the climax, *bam, bash, boom!*
This awful attack is never-ending,
The message is clear in which he's sending,
He's sent many people to their doom.

Suddenly he stopped his rage,
He's shut himself back into his cage,
Now he's silent, soundless, sleepy,
He is no longer sad and weepy.
But only for a time he's reasonably sane,
To be sure, no doubt, it'll happen again . . .

Margaret Ann Macleod (11)
Barvas Primary School, Isle of Lewis

The Tsunami

The tsunami is like a piranha
Barbaric and bloodthirsty
It's as ruthless as a tiger
As sneaky as a spider
Untamed like the great King Kong.

He swirls and twirls all day
Stirring just like a bombing sandstorm
He gnaws into people
Into babies just been born.

He introduces pain into your life
By biting upon your feet
Even in a large river
He'll come to the attack with sharp teeth.

But when the sharky tornadoes come
He'll run away in the distance
Both are 'brothers of destruction'
Killing from the seabed to the shore
But eventually running to bed.

Peter Macaskill (11)
Barvas Primary School, Isle of Lewis

The Tornado

The tornado is like an elephant,
Stampeding away from poachers.
It is unstoppable - *thump, thump, thump!*
It is grey like an old man's hair.

Hither and thither he wreaks havoc,
When it is close to a town
People scream and shout scrambling to escape,
Destroying everything in its path.

After it's gone, chaos all around,
Everything laid bare,
Only when it is safe
Do people and animals venture back.

Suddenly everything is quiet,
The tornado is disappearing as it heads out to sea,
The elephants are calm, they are drinking,
But it is waiting, waiting, waiting
For the next time.

Jonn Norman Macleod (10)
Barvas Primary School, Isle of Lewis

Lightning Tiger

The lightning storm is like a fierce tiger,
Silently searching for its prey,
Striking suddenly and moving swiftly,
It pounces on its victim.

Darting, dashing like an arrow,
Flashing, sabre teeth it growls and grunts,
The antelope is coming closer,
Suddenly he spots the danger,
He bolts and the tiger follows.

They run and run a furious race
The antelope shivers in hopelessness
But finally the tiger gives up the chase
He hears hunters, he spurts and sprints homewards
Tomorrow, undaunted, he will try again.

Catriona Mair (10)
Barvas Primary School, Isle of Lewis

Happiness

Happiness is a yellow sun.
Happiness sounds like a colourful hummingbird
Standing to sing in an enormous tree.
It tastes like very gooey candyfloss
Fluffing and puffing round your tummy
That feels very tickly.
Happiness feels like a soft goodnight kiss on the lips
From my mum.
Happiness smells like beautiful flowers,
With a spectacular bouquet.
Happiness looks like a very cute soft teddy
That I cuddle every night.
Happiness reminds me of playing with my friends
It's so much fun I don't want to stop.

Rachael Smith (8)
Bernera Primary School, Isle of Lewis

Love

Love is soft pink,
An elegant rose bush swaying gently in the breeze.
Love looks like . . .
A white wedding dress,
Floating delicately down a flower-strewn aisle.
Has the taste of
Mountainous helpings of mouth-watering chocolate fudge cake,
Topped with scrumptious cherries and sprinkles.
A passionate kiss on my cheek,
An affectionate hold of my hand.
Love has the enticing aroma,
Delicious freshly baked cookies
With gooey chocolate chips.
Love is a charming and endearing melody of birdsong,
Sweet and soulful music.
Love reminds me of a radiant ballet dancer
Gliding gracefully across a glistening floor,
A swan on a silvery pond.

Ella Macaulay (11)
Bernera Primary School, Isle of Lewis

Anger

Anger is ferocious red like molten lava.
Anger looks like an enormous tsunami striking an island,
The island sinks.
It tastes of piping hot pepperoni pizza
Burning my mouth.
Anger feels like a spiky nettle stinging me,
Itchy, hard, lumpy and red.
Anger smells like a sticky swamp,
Insects and small mammals crawling and scampering everywhere.
The sound of a gigantic wolf ferociously growling at me.
Anger reminds me of terrifying thunder and lightning,
Colliding with a giant tree.

Andrew Macinnes (7)
Bernera Primary School, Isle of Lewis

Jealousy

Jealousy is dark green,
Glaring big bright eyes staring fiercely at you.
Jealousy looks like the swirling deep green fumes of poisonous gas,
Creeping and curling around the room.
Jealousy tastes sickening, like pencil sharpenings,
Jaggy, dry and truly horrific.
Jealousy is warm, slimy, wet hands,
Trying to make you suffer,
Roughly grabbing your neck and choking you.
The sound of someone frightfully screaming in your ear for help,
Which will never stop.
The ghastly intense smell of clumps of rubber,
Burning ferociously in a blazing fire.
Jealousy reminds me of a heart-stopping, terrifying creature,
With dark gleaming skin and horrific eyes,
Which only appears in your nightmares.

Zoe Macinnes (11)
Bernera Primary School, Isle of Lewis

Guilt

Guilt is a dark blue sky.
It looks like a dark well-grown green bush on fire,
Crackling and turning into piles of smoky ash.
The sound of thunder rumbling through your head
And the beat of the snare drum.
Guilt tastes like too much gooey lumpy porridge,
Oaty, heavy and strong.
The feel of your heart thumping so hard,
Pounding in your chest.
Guilt smells like big clouds of smoke from a peat fire,
Puffing up the chimney hole.
Guilt reminds me of times I have hurt someone by accident,
Of when I have done wrong,
Of disobeying.
Guilt is loathsome.

Sarah Maclean (10)
Bernera Primary School, Isle of Lewis

Anger

Anger is a red volcano.
It tastes like the hottest chilli pepper in the world,
Like your mouth is on fire,
Horrible, hot and disgusting.
It smells of water,
That has been in the same place for a hundred years.
It sounds like a really loud tiger
Growling beside your ear.
It looks like your boyfriend is in love with your best friend,
Dump him
And your friend!
It feels like you're going to scream in someone's ear,
Like you're going to throw things,
Like a red-hot volcano is going to erupt on your house,
With red, boiling lava running down on top.
Anger reminds me of hot sizzling ground
And feet that are on fire.

Kiera Greenshields (9)
Bernera Primary School, Isle of Lewis

Excitement

Excitement is violet in the rainbow,
It is a kangaroo jumping up and down
Which never ever stops.
Fizzing Love Hearts that go *fizz, pop, sizzle* and *bang,*
Swirling right round in your mouth.
Quivering jelly that vibrates
And wobbles in my belly.
Chocolate cookies or muffins that smell so delicious,
My tummy rumbles.
Excitement is travelling to London
Going on the London Eye,
Circling around.
Excitement reminds me of Christmas dinner,
All hot and scrumptious.

Jessica Macaulay (7)
Bernera Primary School, Isle of Lewis

Sadness

Sadness is a clear teardrop
Running down your cheeks.
It smells like onions being chopped up
And plonked in spaghetti.
Sadness is a very lonely person
Sitting quietly in a corner.
Sadness feels like you have hurt yourself
On a solid black road
Which is so hard
A lorry could tip over and break.
The sound of someone starting to weep
Loudly in the playground.
Sadness tastes like a drink of water
Flowing down your throat.
It reminds me of my cat getting put down by the vet,
I started to cry.

Euan Gilmour (7)
Bernera Primary School, Isle of Lewis

Excitement

Excitement is a blazing orange.
Excitement looks like a gleaming shooting star,
Someone's eyes so wide open that they are disintegrating.
Excitement sounds like my dog Sam,
Barking rowdily at a car.
A fizzy drink overflowing,
It tastes like a big juicy steak
And ice cream and hot chocolate sauce.
Excitement feels like fluff tickling me.
Smells like a delicious roast chicken
And reminds me of my dog Rusty.

Jonathon Macdonald (8)
Bernera Primary School, Isle of Lewis

Hidden Treasures

When I was walking along the beach,
I saw something I couldn't reach.
It was in the sea, it started to shine,
I put my hand in - it was mine.
It was pretty heavy when I pulled it out,
'It was a treasure chest,' I had to shout.
What was in it? I had to know,
I needed to show my family, I have to go.
But it was too heavy to carry there,
I will have to open it just right here.
But how does it open? There is no key!
I wonder where it can be?
I walked along the stony sand,
The sun was shining on the land.
I looked all around for the key that would fit,
Then finally I found it in a pit.
I put my hand in to pull it out,
But then I started to have my doubt.
It looked just like a piece of metal,
Maybe from an old rusty kettle.
So I thought I might chuck it in the sea,
What good will it be to me?

Eve Maguire (11)
Bressay Primary School, Shetland

Celtic

Celtic is my favourite football team,
I don't have a favourite player,
They are all really good at football and win a lot of matches.
The goalie gets a lot of catches.
They have a good strip
With green and white stripes.
The T-shirts don't rip.
Celtic - they rule!

Nicole Johnston (12)
Bressay Primary School, Shetland

I Like Sports

I like snooker and pool
Because they are fun
I like to pot the colours
All the colours of the world.

I like football
I play it with my friends
And I go to football practise on Tuesday
And that is why I like it.

I like running
I can run as fast as the wind
I like to race against other people
I like to run with my dog.

Ross Maciver (9)
Carloway Primary School, Isle of Lewis

Countries

There's lots of different countries
Like the UK, Japan and Holland
But the UK is made from a few
England, Wales, Ireland and Scotland
America is one of the biggest
And very, very rich
And Canada is very large too
I heard they have a witch!
Russia is very big
Its capital is Moscow
It can be very, very cold
I wonder if they have a shop called Cosco.

Andrew Macleod (9)
Carloway Primary School, Isle of Lewis

My Friends

My friends are small and tall
Ages 7, 8, 9 and 10
Dark hair, blonde hair, long hair, short hair
Big eyes, small eyes, brown and blue eyes

Football, pool and PlayStation
That's the games we play
Our favourite one is football
Which we play every day

My friends are the best ever
I do not know what I would do without them
We play games every day
We are good friends.

Joseph Armstrong (9)
Carloway Primary School, Isle of Lewis

My Gran

My gran is the best
But my mum says she's a pest
She's old and batty, like a bat
But I still love her.

My gran's called Mary
She's really very scary
Sometimes my gran plays tricks on me
But I still love her.

My gran lives near my house
She's as quiet as a mouse
I don't see her often
But I still love her.

Annie Macleod (10)
Carloway Primary School, Isle of Lewis

My Dog

My dog is called Fido
He is an English springer spaniel
We got him a year ago
We got him in Uig.

He runs about like mad
So mad he is like a headless chicken
He loves to be played with
And likes to be walked.

He has chewed a chair
And ripped wallpaper down
He eats, plays, sleeps and goes mad each day
He likes his food a lot.

He drinks and drinks after running
He has also wrecked the garden
He likes to get rubbed under his tummy
And when he gets excited he does the toilet.

My dog is a male dog
He is still a puppy and crazy
But most of all he is a cute puppy
And he has never bitten anyone.

He has black and white hair
And the longest ears
And the biggest eyes
And he has monster claws.

He has big monster teeth
To chew through thick wood
But he is the best puppy
In the whole *world!*

Mark Macleod (11)
Carloway Primary School, Isle of Lewis

Bess!

My dog Bess is very friendly
She never bites or jumps on you
My dog Bess never makes a mess
She is as fast as the wind
My dog Bess loves going for a walk.

My dog Bess adores chasing the sheep
She would play with you until she faints
My dog Bess sleeps without barking
And I think she is the *best!*

She is a black and white collie
With a very shiny coat
She eats dog food and when she is good
She gets a bone.

She will take the bone
And hide it in the ground
And when she is hungry
She will dig it up again.

She is our fourth dog
And she is very nice
With her bone in her mouth
And her shiny, shiny coat.

She will play with you all day.

Alexander Maciver (11)
Carloway Primary School, Isle of Lewis

My Family

I am the second youngest in my family
There are nine people altogether
With two older sisters and three older brothers
The youngest one is nine years old.

She is small and happy
With a smile across her face
She giggles and she laughs
All day long.

My oldest brother is twenty-five
He is tall and friendly
When you are sad he will cheer you up
By giving you a hug and keeps you warm.

My oldest sister is eighteen
She is nice and cuddly
She has lovely brown eyes
And long brown hair.

The others are special too
They all look the same
But inside they are very different
They are nice, happy and very comforting.

My parents are really cool
I don't know how I would live without them
They are both short so that explains everything
But the smaller the better.

Well that's my family for you
The best you can ever get
That's all I can tell you
So bye till the next time.

Kirsteen MacMillan (11)
Carloway Primary School, Isle of Lewis

My Pet Rabbit

I love my rabbit
Her name is Topsey
She is black
With a cute little nose.

I love Topsey
Because she is all mine
Even though she ate Mum's rose.

Topsey is so cute
I love her no matter what
I chase her and play with her outside in the sunshine.

She is so mischievous
But I still love her.

She is small, she is cute
And she is black
Like the dark night sky
She bites you
But only if you annoy her
And she growls too
She jumps up on your legs
If you are wearing a dressing gown.

She has got small, cute, brown eyes
Just like me
She likes to attack my mum's slippers
She plays with my cats
But they are scared of her.

My family thinks
She is really cute
But not as much as I do
I bought her myself.

I love Topsey.

Kathryn MacMillan (9)
Carloway Primary School, Isle of Lewis

Time Machine

I went into my time machine,
I flicked the switches, spun the dials.
I'm going to go for miles and miles into the past,
Now watch out for that spinning vortex blast.
Here I go, it's so exciting, in fact it's nail-biting,
Where am I going? What am I going to do?
I'll pick something simple like cavemen or knights,
But it is so hard to pick a time period - pre-historic or medieval.
I'll pick something quick before I land like a brick.
I'll pick I were in medieval times and I were a king.
Zip, bang, whoosh, this time machine is faster than a cheetah.
Here I am at the round table and on me there's a label,
It's big, it's yellow, it has writing.
I read it quick it says:
'Dear King,
Ye forgot ye were hosting the knight's feast tonight.
Your squire Daylon'.

Oh no I've got to think fast, what shall I do?
I know I'll call my servants and put up a royal banquet.
Wait, what's happening?
I'm hurling through time and space.
Aww, I'm back in my time machine,
Oh well, time to go and see what Mum's cooking.

Ewan Macleod (9)
Carloway Primary School, Isle of Lewis

Inside My Wardrobe

Inside my wardrobe it's a magic place,
It's my secret base,
I go there every night,
Only when no one's in sight.

Inside my wardrobe there are knights and crooks
And a couple of French cooks,
There are ghouls and ghosts
Which came from the coat.

Inside my wardrobe there is a moody princess,
Well if you were locked in a tower wouldn't you feel stressed?
There are talking animals and seven small dwarfs,
Who meet with aliens and their leader Morphs.

Inside my wardrobe there are dancing fish
Who always sing about their favourite dish,
When the dinner is over we party all night long,
Until we hear the clock go *bong!*

The sun comes up,
I run back to bed,
Just in time for Mum
To come in my room and say,
'School time!'

Anne Macleod (10)
Carloway Primary School, Isle of Lewis

Amazing Animals

An octopus flew past my window
A clownfish ran down the street
A sea cucumber rang, said his name was Boe!
A jellyfish limped over my feet.

An elephant was *wanted* for doing ballet
A giraffe was almost touching the sky
A tiger was swimming my way
A warthog was trying its hardest to fly.

An owl was sniffing chocolate-covered hay
A chicken was licking sheep food
A donkey was eating curds and whey
A goat was chewing toilet paper and not being good.

An orang-utan was pruning his plumage
A giant millipede had only one leg
A snake was eating all its luggage
A tarantula was growing five heads.

Elgin Sammons (11)
Carloway Primary School, Isle of Lewis

My Dog Minni

Makes me glad when I'm sad
You'll still love her if she's been bad

Cute and cuddly is how she's described
Oh how I love her soft white hair
Outside sniffing new smells in the garden
Loves to chew socks and chase the cat

Makes you feel very safe at all times
Is always happy to go on a walk
Never bites or barks at anyone
Nice and kind to everyone she knows
Is very small but very fast.

Ryan Macleod (11)
Carloway Primary School, Isle of Lewis

My Great Family

M um is really bossy but always in a good mood
Y ou'd love my dad if you'd ever meet him

G randad and Granny are always caring towards us
R eally great, I don't know what I'd do without them
E veryone gets on well with one another
A unties and uncles are always kind to us
T ender and thoughtful every day

F ights with my brother never last long
A lways teaching us to be fair to one another
M agic to have such a fun loving family
I ncredible cousins to talk to and visit
L oving, considerate and helpful to others
Y ou'd be lucky if you had a family like mine.

Cameron Macarthur (11)
Carloway Primary School, Isle of Lewis

Sport Is Fun

S ome people are good, some are bad
P eople play them every day
O n the land, on the sea or in the air
R ound the world we all love to play
T ogether we play to win the cups

I love sport because it keeps me fit and healthy
S ometimes it can cause a fight but it's just a game

F ootball, fishing and racing
U sually is what I love to do
N ice and exciting.

Glenn Macarthur (9)
Carloway Primary School, Isle of Lewis

Emma Lee Is My Niece

E mma Lee is small
M akes a lot of noise
M ornings are the worst
A lways crying for food.

L ikes listening to The Beatles
E veryone wants to hold her
E verything loud scares her.

I love holding her
S he always gives me a sweet smile.

M akes me laugh
Y awns a lot.

N ight-time is the best
I n her cot she sleeps soundly
E xcellent at drinking her milk
C ute and cuddly
E mma Lee is the best.

Rory Macdonald (9)
Carloway Primary School, Isle of Lewis

Superdog

Superdog fell in a toxic barrel,
Now he speaks French, English and Welsh.
He is Superman's best friend.
He shoots laser beams from his eyes.
He is as fast as lightning.
He is as strong as an ox.
He is as smart as a dolphin.
Superdog is one cool Dalmatian.
Superdog always catches the robbers,
He has a case full of medals.
Superdog, Superdog, what a dog!
No wonder he's New York's favourite dog.

Gary Carmichael
Carloway Primary School, Isle of Lewis

Monsters

Monsters give you a huge big fright,
Especially on a dark night.
Monsters are big, ugly and tall,
To go near one you would have to be a really big fool.
If you dared to enter their cave,
You would be classed as really brave.
Their homes are oh so dark and damp,
To light them up you would need a really big lamp.
When you approach them you get a cold shiver of fear,
Then you think, *why did I even come here?*
When he sees you he goes boo
And then you run away screaming, 'What am I going to do?'
Monsters are so very big,
But when they get old they shrivel up like a fig.
Monsters can smell your fear,
So don't be scared and treat them like an old dear.
All your friends just run away,
But you don't, you just stay.
But when he sees you,
You wish you had run away too.
You run away but it's no good,
He'll just come after you with his big hood.
Monsters, monsters, they love eating,
But someone should give them a beating.
Everyone just runs away before they even get to know him,
But maybe he has feelings and a name like Tim.
Everyone must be blind,
Because really the monster is really kind.

Seumas Beathan (10)
Carloway Primary School, Isle of Lewis

Green

Green is the colour of the grass
In my big, big garden.
Green is the colour of my bedroom
In my nice big house.
Green is the colour of the Celtic top
On all the Celtic players.
Green is the colour of a grasshopper
In the long dewy grass.
Green is the colour of a crocodile
With its *snappy, snappy* jaws!

Innes Macleod (9)
Carloway Primary School, Isle of Lewis

Winter Poem

Icy grass feels cold
Frozen hands making snowballs
Gales of snow making me cold
Jack Frost covering the cars in ice.

Harry Cartwright (6)
Cullivoe Primary School, Shetland

I'm Not Frightened, Not Me!

Pumpkins with big scary teeth,
Bats flapping with their wings,
Skeletons with no skin on,
I'm not frightened, not me!

Witches turning people into frogs,
Ghosts chasing people upstairs,
Vampires with spiky teeth,
I'm not frightened, not me!

Kyle Williamson (5)
Cullivoe Primary School, Shetland

I'm Not Frightened, Not Me!

Poisonous slimy jellyfish
Trying to sting me,
Good for jellyfish jam,
I'm not frightened, not me!

Vampires with sharp teeth,
Black cloaks flapping,
Wanting me for supper,
I'm not frightened, not me!

Witches with a pointy hat,
Flying on their brooms,
Casting a magic spell,
I'm not frightened, not me!

Thunder and lightning trying to strike me,
Ghosts with no skin trying to get me,
Bats flying in the moonlit sky,
I'm not frightened, not me!

Ethan Peel (6)
Cullivoe Primary School, Shetland

My Winter Poem

Snowflakes twinkling in the sky,
Children eating Christmas pie,
People shivering in the snow,
Icicles swaying to and fro,
Everybody in the sleet,
All the children having cold feet,
Snow is lots and lots of fun,
But soon it will melt in the sun.

Brodie Lawson (8)
Cullivoe Primary School, Shetland

The Dragon

The dragon lay in his cave,
Along came a knight, the knight was brave.
The dragon stood up and hit the knight,
He then breathed fire and set the cave alight.
The knight knew he had to escape,
So he stabbed the dragon but the dragon went ape.
The rest of the villagers went up to see
The dragon breaking the knight's left knee.
The dragon ended up killing the knight
And that was the end of the horrific fight.
But the rest of the villagers can't give up,
They stood outside the cave and lined up.
Each of them threw a very sharp knife,
Most of them hit the dragon and ended the dragon's life.

Jack Lawson (11)
Cullivoe Primary School, Shetland

Going To The Pantomime

I am glad that I am going to the pantomime,
I can't wait to see magic and much, much more,
I am looking forward to seeing baddies and goodies in the show,
The magic cave will be enchanting,
Watching it on seats in the theatre,
Getting scared when the lights go dim for the baddies,
Feeling happy when the goodies win
And clapping at the end of the show,
Waiting for the curtain to close.

Daniel Franklin (9)
Cullivoe Primary Schoo!, Shetland

Untitled

Pegasus glittering in the sky above,
A swoop on the rainbow is as easy as dust,
Her wings are as white as snow,
Her furry coat is as pink as rose,
If I were up with her I would go to Alaska
And see the monsters stamp,
I would like to go to a fairytale land
And see where the chocolate things grow,
But the thing I want most of all is to go to a chocolate home.

Ming Sandford (7)
Cullivoe Primary School, Shetland

I'm Not Frightened, Not Me!

A zombie in the dark,
I'm not frightened, not me!

A vampire sucking blood,
I'm not frightened, not me!

Cats fighting, howling and screeching,
I'm not frightened, not me!

Skeletons rattling their bones,
I'm not frightened, not me!

Joseph Edmondson (11)
Cullivoe Primary School, Shetland

Fairies

Fairies glittery,
Fairies flying in the sky,
With the rainbow in the sky,
Dancing everywhere.

Sarah Thomason (5)
Cullivoe Primary School, Shetland

Winter

I quite like snow
I like snowflakes falling down
Covering the ground
It looks like a white blanket
Children running
Falling down
Making snow angels
Then having a snowball fight.

Louise Thomason (7)
Cullivoe Primary School, Shetland

Winter Poem

Hailstones tumbling to the ground
Kids sledging down a hill
Jack Frost making all the cars frosty
Robins flying in the sky
Kids building snowmen in snow
Icicles hanging from the roof
I really love winter.

Calvin Brown (9)
Cullivoe Primary School, Shetland

Eoligarry

E oligarry is where I live
O ver a hill
L ovely beaches
I nstant fun
G reat neighbours
A nd great friends
R eally great
R eally fun
Y ou should come along.

Ryan MacNeil (11)
Eoligarry Primary School, Isle of Barra

Isle Of Barra

I love Barra
S hopkeepers are nice
L ove is shared
E veryone is kind.

O ran is my name
F amily and friends are nice.

B oats go out the bay
A urora-B was my dad's boat
R olls all over the sea
R oads are clean
A ll the shops are small.

Oran Boyd (8)
Eoligarry Primary School, Isle of Barra

Isle Of Barra

I live on an island
S omewhere on the west of Scotland
L ike it there
E ven though it rains

O ver the hills the birds
F lying in the sky

B eautiful place
A lways shining
R ainbows in the sky
R eally nice
A small place but beautiful.

Kristie Boyd (9)
Eoligarry Primary School, Isle of Barra

My Brother And I

My brother and I always argue,
My brother and I always shout,
But my brother and I love each other
And of that I have no doubt.

I think my brother is crazy,
I think my brother is mad,
I know my brother is lazy
And to say that I feel pretty glad.

My brother and I stick together,
Whenever something gets rough,
I believe I am a genius
And he thinks that he is tough . . . as if!

My brother is tall and so am I,
But he's so tall he could touch the sky,
He's got big clumpy feet
And I am just sweet,
So that's my brother and I.

Annemarie MacNeil (11)
Eoligarry Primary School, Isle of Barra

Jack-In-A-Box

Jack, jack, jack-in-a-box
Jack, jack, jack-in-a-box
Where have you gone jack-in-a-box?
Where have you gone?
Come to play
Where have you gone jack-in-a-box?
Where have you gone?
Jack, jack, pop out of your box
Jack, jack, time to play
Jack, jack, come on let's play
Jack, jack, come on let's play.

Alasdair Elder (9)
Eoligarry Primary School, Isle of Barra

Strange Planets

I live on planet Bigenov
Where everyone is small.
Even when we're quite grown up
We're still not very tall.

The flowers are so big and tall
They really are quite scary,
So is the dog that lives next door,
It's really big and hairy!

My friend who owns him is called Mark.
He trained him so he would not bark.
He takes him for a walk each day,
(Or the dog takes him, I ought to say!)

One day when I went out to play
A ladybird got in my way.
Then I hit my ball so far away
I had to search for half the day.

If I could have one wish come true,
I'd like to be as big as you,
I ask, as I look up to the sky,
Why am I so small, oh why?

Michael Mackinnon (10)
Eoligarry Primary School, Isle of Barra

Under The Sea

Under the sea
Where the fish swim,
There's a wreck,
An old boat wreck.
In the wreck there's a shark,
An old friendly shark.
He is really a nice guy,
He just wants to play.
He just wants to be friends,
He is just a nice guy.

Brendon Hart (8)
Eoligarry Primary School, Isle of Barra

Night-Time

Night approaches like a wolf hunting prey.
The darkness creeps out again preparing to cause havoc.

In the dark I see huge frightening shadows.
I hear cars roaring and dogs howling.
I smell only car fumes in the air.
I touch nothing.
I taste my fear coming out of its shell and growing.
I feel trapped and defenceless.

Jasmine Brown (11)
Laxdale Primary School, Isle of Lewis

Anger

Anger is red
Like a fierce bloodthirsty dog.
It sounds like a bunged up engine.
Anger tastes like fiery hot curry.
Anger smells like smoke burning furiously.
Anger looks like my sister when she wakes up in the morning.
Anger feels like sharp thumb tacks.
Anger reminds me of an explosion.

Calum Macdonald (11)
Laxdale Primary School, Isle of Lewis

Darkness

Darkness is pearly-black
Like a dark mysterious shadow.
It sounds like a glass shattering in the night.
It tastes like sour milk.
It smells like smoke in the kitchen.
It looks like a leopard prowling for its prey
And it feels like someone is watching you . . .

Jake Rivett (11)
Laxdale Primary School, Isle of Lewis

Henry VIII

Henry VIII, so big and bold,
But on the inside so hard and cold.
Shouting out orders, just like a tyrant,
Acting the boss, just like a giant.
All the styles, fancy jewellery and clothes
And a big army to fight off his foes.
Lots of big ships, loaded with guns
And ever so desperate for a son.
He wanted everything,
Head of the church
And got terribly fat,
On his royal perch.
Had six wives, one of them stayed,
Jane Seymour, a baby boy she made.
The rest were beheaded, divorced or died,
All because Henry VIII sighed.
He wanted desperately a son,
But none of them would give him one.
Gave him some girls, and then came his star,
His and Jane's marriage really went far.
But all in all Henry was greedy
And didn't care about the poor and needy.
But soon enough all his money was spent
And all his supporters away they went.
England was a country poor
And its inhabitants were quite sure
They were ruined and Henry was bad
But this made him very sad.
So he worked real hard
And got the money back.
People began to cut him some slack
And then Henry VIII went and died
I'm sure most of England cried.
This was the end of Henry's story,
With lots of battles, some quite gory.
And now my poem is done,
Reading it was quite fun.

Erin Donnelly (11)
Laxdale Primary School, Isle of Lewis

Night

The gloomy night sweeps silently drowning the light from in front
of your eyes
Everything is silent, no one's around
It starts to get creepy now the mist has appeared
Cars are speeding past with their headlights lighting their way
as they go
You start to get scared, it's time to go home
Now you're safe and sound in your very own house
Slowly and quietly the night disappears leaving only daylight to see,
wait, what's that!

Mary Jones (11)
Laxdale Primary School, Isle of Lewis

Night-Time

Night-time approaches like a panther hunting down prey.
The night is cheerless, mysterious and gloomy.
I am worried something or someone is lurking behind me.
I hear creaky, strange noises.
When I walk I feel a bitter shiver running down my back.
I see nothing but a flickering light in the distance.
I grip my knuckles and try to rush home but I can't, I'm trapped
I see home, I'm safe.

Ebony Purdham (11)
Laxdale Primary School, Isle of Lewis

The Monster From Mars

There once was a monster from Mars,
Who reached up and grabbed twinkly stars,
He liked to fly to the moon
And eat cheese with a spoon,
But didn't like journeys in space cars.

Lauren Macarthur (11)
Laxdale Primary School, Isle of Lewis

Night-Time

Night-time approaches like a rabbit in a dark hole
Its feet digging more and more
The black starry night is looking down on me.

Night drifts back once again
Like a leopard stalking for its prey
I see nothing but a dark shadow.

I smell nothing, touch nothing, taste nothing.

I feel afraid as it gets darker and darker through the night
I jump at the loud noises I hear through the night
I tremble with fear.

Morning comes like a newborn lamb
I am no longer scared
Everything is calm and clear.

Lorna Morrison (11)
Laxdale Primary School, Isle of Lewis

Are You Scared Of The Dark?

Night-time approaches like an express train going at the speed of light
Scared are all whom are outside at that fearful time of night
The unlit sky, not a star in sight, scary as can be
A wolf howling in the distance frightens all but me
Are you afraid of the dark?
Are you? Are you?
Shadows appearing here and there, boo! Boo!
Dawn has broken, night has gone
Another day to go, until the fearful night will come
And scare off all my foe.

Jessica Ann Macdonald (11)
Laxdale Primary School, Isle of Lewis

Night-Time

Night-time approaches like a black panther hunting for its prey.
The gloomy night sweeps silently, drowning the light
of the flickering candle.
Mysterious people venture around in the streets
as others are feeling safe inside.
In the dark I hear the animals rummaging round in the leaves.
I feel the wind against my face, it is bitterly cold.
I hear leaves rustling among the trees
and dogs barking in the distance.
I can smell burning wood as if a fire has just been lit.
The lamp posts are out and the stillness is spooky.
I can see a black cat prowling along my window sill.
Dawn is now approaching and I am waking up,
no more spooky things or thoughts, I hope,
oh no what's that ?

Erinn Nicolson (11)
Laxdale Primary School, Isle of Lewis

Inside At Night

Night-time approaches like a cat stalking her prey and pounces,
quick and sudden.
In the dark I see nothing, I hear nothing, I smell nothing,
I touch nothing, I taste nothing,
I feel isolated and scared.

The gloomy night sweeps silently, blotting out the light
drowning it slowly like a man swept off a boat
and set plunging into utter darkness and into a cold watery death.

An exasperated monster bursts free from his cage into the light,
the monster is no longer irritated and is now in a blissful mood.

Rachel Campbell (11)
Laxdale Primary School, Isle of Lewis

When Night-Time Approaches

When night-time approaches quickly
Like a coal train moving swiftly
Getting closer and closer every day
It gets bleaker and bleaker
Blacker and blacker like what a stranger would say.

It is like a pure black panther
Hunting for its prey
Slowly and carefully
Trying to dismay
It could pounce at any moment
Roar at any time
Even if you run you still can't hide.

So next time you're out
Be afraid to shout
Because you'll never know what's about!

Catherine Drummond (10)
Laxdale Primary School, Isle of Lewis

Untitled

'Mum, you know the tin of biscuits?'
'Yes.'
'The dog ate them.'
'Mmmm.'
'Baby took them.'
'Right.'
'OK, I tried to stop them but the aliens got away.'
'Go to your room.'
'OK, the Devil came to tea and ate them all.'
'The truth now.'
'I took them to school and shared them out.'
'You should have told me.'

Tamla Cunningham (10)
North Bute Primary School, Isle of Bute

Waste Of Breath

'Mum, you know your watch? The one you got as a wedding gift.'
'Yes, what about it?'
'Well, I think this morning when we were asleep, someone stole it.'
'Don't talk rubbish - who and how could someone get in here?'
'Santa, through the chimney.'
'What? It is the middle of summer for crying out loud.'
'Maybe he was on a vacation.'
'Yes of course, oh! I just remembered I saw Rudolph in Valencia.'
'Really!'
'What age are you?'
'11.'
'Well can you please act it?'
'OK!'
'Anyway, why did you bring this up?'
'I don't know.'
'Tell the truth.'
'There is no truth.'
'Yes there is and if you don't tell me the truth, I will shoot
the boots off you.'
'OK! OK! OK! What happened was I *accidentally* dropped it
and it broke, that's 100% truth, OK?'
'No, that's far from OK.'

Joe Livingstone (11)
North Bute Primary School, Isle of Bute

Excuses

'Mum, you know those flowers you love? They have gone missing.'
'Is that the truth?'
'Well Jack ate them.'
'Really now.'
'Some cows ran through the house and took them.'
'The truth or no pocket money.'
'Fine. They died and I put them in the bin.'

Robert Deans (10)
North Bute Primary School, Isle of Bute

Where Is My Chocolate?

'Dad, you know the huge bar of chocolate you bought?
Well it's gone.'
'Where?'
'I think the cat and the dog kind of ate it last night.'
'The cat and dog can't open the cupboard, so tell the truth.'
'Superman came in the window and ate it all.'
'Come on cough it up.'
'Little gnomes came in the window and bombed the chocolate,
told you they were evil.'
'Tell me the truth or I'll ground you for a year.'
'Well . . . '
'Cat got your tongue?'
'Yes, actually, get it off!
Well I kind of ate it all but it was very nice.'

Matthew Dunn (11)
North Bute Primary School, Isle of Bute

Identity

Born on September the 12th
Just luckily not the 11th
My best friend is Deanna
We have known each other since nursery
My favourite food is chicken, peas, carrots, roast potatoes
I hate leeches, they are just so creepy and yucky
I love my family
I am very shy

But

If I had the chance to be anything I'd be . . . a parrot
With lovely colourful feathers
Repeat my fave words
Fly and amuse people, sing my fave songs.

Katelyn Gordon (10)
North Bute Primary School, Isle of Bute

Identity

My name is Georgina
I was born on March 14th 1995
My favourite subject is animals
I hate spiders and daddy-long-legs
I have a big family and some I don't know about
I like spaghetti Bolognese
I hate macaroni cheese
I like hamsters and dogs
I love to cook and draw
I like fruit and veg.

But

If I could be anything
I would be a . . . duck
I would swim as far as I want to go
I would have lovely warm feathers
And play with other ducks
Then I would have little baby ducklings.

Georgina Toft (11)
North Bute Primary School, Isle of Bute

Identity

My name is Scott
I love Scotch pie
Nice, soft, crispy with mince
My favourite place is Cyprus
Because it is hot

But

If I could be anything I wanted to be . . .
I'd be a ferret
I could eat fish especially mackerel
I could fight and I could climb
And eat rabbits
And keep fit when I go hunting.

Scott Dunn (9)
North Bute Primary School, Isle of Bute

Identity

I love guinea pigs.
I have two guinea pigs
Called Willow and Rusty.
I hate cockroaches.
I saw a cockroach in Canada
As big as a frog!

But . . .

If I could be anything
I would be a . . . Highland cow.
I would be very fat and strong
I would get groomed at a show and win a rosette
I would get loads of food
I would be very scary
And people would run away from me.
Mooo!

Lewis MacMillan (10)
North Bute Primary School, Isle of Bute

What Happened To The Apple Pie?

'Mum, see that apple pie you made for dessert, well it's gone.'
'Where has it gone?'
'The dog ate it.'
'Be honest.'
'OK, Gran came round and ate it.'
'Deanna?'
'OK, Superman came and stole it.'
'Come on?'
'It flew away.'
'Really?'
'OK, I got hungry and I ate it.'

Deanna MacDonald (10)
North Bute Primary School, Isle of Bute

Excuses

'Mum, you know the caravan? Well, it's gone.'
'Where has it gone?'
'I think a crow came and flew away with it.'
'No, what happened?'
'Actually the doctor said it was unsafe
and that he had to take it away.'
'It wasn't unsafe, so tell me what happened.'
'OK, Batman swooped down and took it away.'
'So Batman came from outer space
and just happened to take the caravan?'
'Someone from France came and bought it and took it home.'
'Yeah right.'
'Next-door's sheep came with their suitcases
and took the caravan to Spain.'
'Tell the truth otherwise I'll ground you for three months.'
'Fine, my friends and I were playing and the hitch was loose
and I fell onto the hitch and it came undone
and it rolled down the hill.'
'Well, that's fine but you didn't have to tell all those silly lies.'

Elizabeth Mellish (11)
North Bute Primary School, Isle of Bute

My Grandpa

My grandpa likes mint humbugs
My grandpa likes pea soup
He likes to read the paper
He'd love an ice cream scoop

He likes to watch the telly
It's usually the news
But when he's in his armchair
He mostly likes to snooze.

Jessie Docherty (10)
North Bute Primary School, Isle of Bute

Excuses

'Lauran, get down here right now.'
'Yes Mum.'
'Why are there books everywhere?'
'Well the dog messed it up.'
'Really!'
'OK Charlie set a trap to scare me.'
'Charlie is a parrot.'
'Superman flew in and had a party.'
'Superman is a comic book hero.'
'A burglar came in and tried to copy my homework.'
'You don't have any homework.'
'Bart Simpson ran in to hide from Principal Skinner.'
'Bart Simpson is a cartoon.'
'Santa Claus came early and when he landed on the roof
the books came out the bookcase.'
'Tell the truth or no swimming for a month.'
'OK, OK, I was dancing to my favourite song
and I fell into the bookshelf.'
'Right, no more music for two months and you're grounded
for one week and clean all the books right *nowww!'*

Lauran Masterson (10)
North Bute Primary School, Isle of Bute

The Missing Chocolate Cake

'What happened to the chocolate cake Mum?'
'Well it's gone.'
'Where has it gone?'
'Dad ate it.'
'Tell the truth.'
'OK, my friend came in and ate it.'
'Leanne!'
'Just tell the truth.'
'OK.
I ate it with my friend.'

Leanne Chisholm (11)
North Bute Primary School, Isle of Bute

Excuses

'Mum, remember the TV that was in your bedroom, well I think the dog knocked it down.'
'You what!'
'Well actually baby Charley pushed it over.'
'Ahem.'
'OK, OK, Superman borrowed it and won't give me it back.'
'Spill.'
'Fine, the cat went on a date with it.'
'If you don't tell me the truth I'll . . . '
'OK I'm sorry, I couldn't stop him.'
'Who?'
'The Devil.'
'Right that's it, you're not getting your pocket money for a month.'
'Fine, OK, I'll tell you, I broke it by *accident.'*

Jade Elizabeth Peters (10)
North Bute Primary School, Isle of Bute

My Alien

The alien I met was disgusting and vile,
It was ugly, fat, round with a revolting smile.
It had a spiky head which could shoot fire,
It was never truthful, always a liar.
It was pretty tall, 5.2 feet,
So ugly and gooey *him* you wouldn't want to meet.
It had six gooey tentacles, bogey-green,
It was smelly, noisy and terribly mean.
Its feet stuck to the ground as he walked,
It groaned and never talked.
My alien, I will never forget,
But one thing is sure *him* I'm glad I met!

Catriona Fyfe (11)
Paible School, North Uist

My Poem

The alien's green
The alien's small
It's not like me
Not at all

The alien's slim
Not skin and bones
It's not like me
It's got three toes

Its favourite food
Is Joshua soup
I should know
It told me so

It pounces on frogs
And gobbles them up
I should know
It told me so.

Barry Ferrol (11)
Paible School, North Uist

My Alien

The alien from outer space was small
With a silly green face
It had a big hairy mole
And liked to eat coal

It had white shiny teeth
It was a thief
It had four eyes
And told a lot of lies

It had spiky blue hair
It didn't really care
It was as vicious as a bear.

Fraser Macdonald (11)
Paible School, North Uist

My Alien Poem

It has lots of slime
When you look at it all the time
And when it is around
There is no crime
What is it?

It has no legs
Just lots of pegs
With some dangly arms
What is it?

It lives in space
With its suitcase
It has a slow pace
What is it?

Millicent Morrell Baines (9)
Paible School, North Uist

My Alien

The alien in space was ace
A spear that looked like his rear
Green goo spread all over his face
Black wax dangling from his ear

Blood dripping from his head
He thought that he was dead
When he sang his tongue rang
He read some books
He got caught in hooks
When he touched his spear it stung and rung.

Ruairidh MacDonald (11)
Paible School, North Uist

My Alien Poem

My alien is green and is ugly,
My alien, his name is Dudley.
My alien has a hairy chest,
My alien is a real pest.

My alien, it really likes me,
My alien, it has green pee.
My alien, it doesn't like my sister,
My alien, he's a cool mister.

My alien has warts on its nose,
My alien, its mouth was zipped closed.
My alien is Dudley McGool,
My alien is just so, so cool!

Fazel Froughi & Calum MacRitchie (9)
Paible School, North Uist

My Alien Poem

The very first alien I was to see
Was long and gangly with a wart on his knee.
Unlike a human it ate lots of slugs
But when I looked closely it ate any sort of bug.

It sat there grinning up at me
But it looked suspicious because it drunk lots of tea.
It had long dark gooey-looking teeth,
Its face looked like a squished slab of beef.

Well that's the story of my alien friend,
Goodbye, farewell, that is the end.

Nicky Spears (10)
Paible School, North Uist

Young Writers Information

We hope you have enjoyed reading this book - and that you will continue to enjoy it in the coming years.

If you like reading and writing poetry drop us a line, or give us a call, and we'll send you a free information pack.

Alternatively if you would like to order further copies of this book or any of our other titles, then please give us a call or log onto our website at www.youngwriters.co.uk

Young Writers Information
Remus House
Coltsfoot Drive
Peterborough
PE2 9JX

(01733) 890066